HERITAGE UNLOCKED

Guide to free sites in Bristol, Gloucestershire and Wiltshire

Bradford-on-Avon Tithe Barn, Wiltshire

CONTENTS

An area of myth, legend and magical scenery, the Bristol, Gloucestershire and Wiltshire region has a number of major attractions such as the World Heritage Site of Stonehenge – but it has a far greater number of English Heritage sites to which entry is completely free. This guidebook is one of a series covering the whole country and provides a concise but informative introduction to each of these sites. Varying from fascinating earthworks dating back thousands of years to the remains of some of the country's most prestigious religious foundations, these diverse sites reflect the long and important history of this region. Among the earliest are the incredible Silbury Hill and Avebury Stone Circles which may have been used for ritual and social purposes and are part of an enormous prehistoric landscape whose mysteries are still being explored.

The Romans established their provincial capital, Corinium (Cirencester) in Gloucestershire and a large amphitheatre was built close by, as well as many impressive villas such as Great Witcombe. The region's later history is reflected in the imposing remains of castles and abbeys reflecting the wealth and power of the monastic orders and dominant local families such as the Berkeleys.

Throughout the book, special features highlight particular aspects of the region; the range of Cotswold Severn long barrows, for example, and some of the writers and artists who have been inspired by its landscape. The sites are described in alphabetical order within each county and, for those who want to see more, a brief guide to English Heritage's paying sites is also given at the end of the book. This guide aims to encourage visitors to explore, understand and enjoy some of the lesser-known – but no less intriguing – monuments in English Heritage's care.

Crypt of St John the Baptist, Bristol

BRISTOL

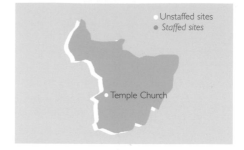

Unstaffed sites
Staffed sites

Temple Church

Exploration and technical innovation are the trademarks of the ancient port of Bristol. In 1497 John Cabot sailed from Bristol aboard the *Matthew* to the New World. In the 19th century, Isambard Kingdom Brunel designed the Clifton Suspension Bridge and his SS *Great Britain*, the first iron-hulled ship, was built here. A century later Concorde, the world's first supersonic airliner was

developed and built at Filton Airfield, Bristol.

The wealth derived from the city's thriving international trade and engineering industries also left a superb architectural legacy – from splendid medieval churches to elegant

Left: Temple Church

Right: Royal York Terrace, Clifton

Georgian crescents, and from the impressive waterfront warehouses to the highly ornate yet functional Victorian engineering of Brunel's Temple Meads railway station.

The famous diarist, Samuel Pepys, described Bristol as 'in every respect another London' – an accolade the city continues to deserve today.

*Clifton Suspension Bridge
completed in 1864*

Bristol's distinctive architectural character reflects its long history and commercial development. The present city was probably begun in the 10th century and fifteen churches of medieval foundation remain. The Cathedral, formerly St Augustine's Abbey, dates from 1140 and has a Norman Chapter House, and particularly fine early 14th-century Decorated work in the Choir. St Mary Redcliffe was largely rebuilt in the 14th century, forming undoubtedly England's most ambitious parish church, on a cruciform plan with full clerestory, spectacular stone vaulting and a 292 ft (89 m) spire. Other highlights include the Norman nave at St James; the majestic tower and interior at St Stephen, *c*1470s; St John, which incorporates a city gate, and has wonderfully complete furnishings of *c*1620–30; and St Mark, or the Lord Mayor's Chapel, where there are rich monuments and Continental Renaissance stained glass.

During the 17th century trade with the American colonies grew dramatically, and the slave trade became central to Bristol's economy. The city is rich in 17th-century timber-framed houses, notably the handsome pub called the Llandoger Trow in King Street. Other interesting examples can be seen in Victoria Street and St Michael's Hill.

Above: Bristol from the top of the Robinson Building
Right: Auditorium of the Theatre Royal

villas such as Royal Fort House, c1758–61, and magnificent and solid Greek Revival terraces such as Vyvyan Terrace, 1833–45, and Worcester Terrace, c1847–53. Less well-known but equally worthwhile is Georgian Kingsdown: from the airy heights around Kingsdown Parade, narrow cobbled lanes plunge down to King Square.

Corn Street, Bristol's old commercial heart, boasts John Wood the Elder's magnificent Palladian Exchange of 1741–3, now a vibrant market. Here too are the best Victorian palaces of commerce, notably Lloyds Bank, 1854–7,

Queen Square, 1699–c1727, reflects the London fashion for classical brick architecture, and No 29, now a regional office of English Heritage, is especially fine. Clifton developed after 1700 from a hilltop hamlet to a fashionable resort for visitors to the Hot Wells spa in the Avon Gorge. There are elegant Georgian merchants'

Top left: Lloyd's Bank, Corn Street
Top right: Victorian stained glass window in St Mary Redcliffe
Right: The north porch vault of St Mary Redcliffe

opposite the Exchange, with riotous carving based loosely on St Mark's Library, Venice. The best 19th-century warehouses are Bush House, Narrow Quay (now the Arnolfini Gallery), 1830–6, and the Granary, Welsh Back – a Byzantine-style layer cake of multi-coloured brick of 1869. Sir George Oatley's Wills Memorial Tower, Queen's Road, 1912–25, for the University of Bristol, is perhaps the last great essay in the English

Left: English Heritage's South-West office in Queen Square
Above: Arnolfini Gallery
Right: Worcester Terrace

Gothic Revival, of the 20th century but wholly Victorian in intent. It is memorably sited and of monumental proportions.

In Bristol the old tended not to be swept away, but adapted to meet changing economic and social requirements. After 1800 the city quickly lost ground to its northern industrial rivals: the relative decrease of wealth was partly responsible for the survival of so much. Despite the depredations of the blitz and post-war demolitions, perhaps nowhere else in Britain can one find such extraordinary variety in the compass of a couple of square miles.

Above: Five centuries of building in King Street
Right: Norman carving in the Chapter House of Bristol Cathedral

History

Bristol's Temple Church is so called because the original church was built by the Knights Templar, perhaps the most famous of the medieval military orders. Founded in the early 12th century to protect pilgrims in the Holy Land, the Templars were 'warrior monks', obeying religious vows of chastity and poverty whilst trained for war.

Temple Church with its amazing leaning tower

Robert, Earl of Gloucester, donated the site of the church to the Templars in the mid-12th century. The original building was round, deliberately recalling the Church of the Holy Sepulchre that stands in Jerusalem. It was one of the largest of only a dozen such churches in England and it appears that the Bristol Temple became the administrative centre for the order in the south-west. By 1307, however, the order had fallen into disrepute and their lands were later confiscated and handed to the Knights Hospitaller.

When the Knights Hospitaller were themselves suppressed by Henry VIII 1540, the church was taken over by the parish. In the 18th century the interior was refitted. The church was bombed during the Second World War and gutted by the resulting

fire. This enabled the site to be excavated and the plan of the former Templar church was revealed. Among the treasures rescued from the debris was a unique medieval chandelier, now in Bristol Cathedral.

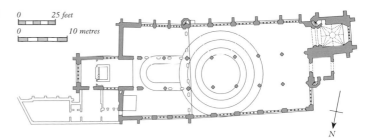

Description

Only the shell of the building, dating mainly from the 14th century, remained after the bombing in 1940. The Hospitallers replaced the older nave with a more spacious rectangular one with side aisles. The shape of the original Templar church is marked out on the ground. The chancel is exceptionally long and flanked by the chapel of St Nicholas to the north, and the chapel of St Catherine to the south. The sombre concrete reinforcements were built following the fire damage to prevent the east end of the nave collapsing. To the west of the nave the Georgian doorway still survives, although the arcades had to be removed as they were unsafe.

The famous tower, which leans 5 ft (1.6 m) out of the vertical, was begun in the 1390s, when the lower three stages were constructed. Work was halted when the tower began to lean but was optimistically resumed *c*1460 when the tall top stage was added with a deliberate correction of the leaning angle (ie the masons tried to build a true vertical stage on top of the leaning base). The top stage is not now vertical, probably due to the fact that the base has continued to increase its lean.

Above: Plan of the Temple Church showing the position of the earlier Templar church

Left: A Knight Templar depicted in a 14th-century manuscript

In Temple Street, Bristol

Open: exterior only, any reasonable time

OS Map 172; ref ST 593727

11

GLOUCESTERSHIRE

The county has three distinct landscapes and some of the most beautiful scenery in England. To the east, the high ground of the Cotswolds is dotted with picturesque villages built from the local honey-coloured limestone on the proceeds of the wool trade. To the west, the ancient Forest of Dean stretches to the Welsh border. In between lie the fertile plains of the Severn valley, the Regency spa town of Cheltenham and the city of Gloucester with its restored docks and magnificent cathedral. The area has long proved attractive to settlers, as demonstrated by impressive Neolithic long barrows, the remains of Roman country villas and many fine medieval churches.

Unstaffed sites
Staffed sites

St Mary's Church, Kempley
Odda's Chapel
Hailes Abbey
Belas Knap Long Barrow
Notgrove Long Barrow
Over Bridge
Blackfriars & Greyfriars
Great Witcombe Roman Villa
St Briavel's Castle
Nympsfield Long Barrow
Cirencester Amphitheatre
Offa's Dyke
Uley Long Barrow
Windmill Tump Long Barrow
Kingswood Abbey Gatehouse

Left: The Cotswold village of Snowshill
Below: Kingswood Abbey Gatehouse
Facing page: The famous Neptune fountain in Cheltenham

Gloucestershire contains one of the most important collections of Neolithic burial monuments in the country. These tombs consist of long stone mounds containing a number of burial chambers, usually entered from passages opening from the sides or ends of the mounds. Roughly seventy such mounds, or long barrows, are known from the county and these belong to a regional distribution known as the 'Cotswold Severn' group which appear to have been constructed between 4000 and 3000 BC.

Above: A Cotswold Severn barrow
Right: Neolithic bowl excavated from a barrow at Hazleton

All the long barrows within Gloucestershire are found in the limestone uplands, usually above the 394 ft (120 m) contour, and there are concentrations around Swell, Bisley and Avening. Although there is variation in the size of these barrows (they can measure between 98 ft (30 m) and 394 ft (120 m) in length), they share common architectural features. The majority of Cotswold long barrows face east and consist of carefully constructed trapezoidal mounds over the stone burial chambers, frequently faced by a drystone wall. The eastern end of the mound is generally higher and wider and usually has two projecting 'horns' on each side creating an entrance forecourt. Mounds with burial chambers in the eastern end are considered to be 'terminally chambered' and may contain between one and five burial chambers. Typically, these chambers are box-like structures arranged in pairs on each side of the passage.

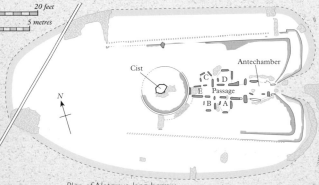

Plan of Notgrove long barrow

A second type of chamber arrangement is known from the Cotswold region. In this case passages lead from the side of the mound into burial chambers and are known to be 'laterally chambered' monuments. Passages usually occur in opposed pairs, on each side of the mound. Both arrangements appear to be roughly contemporary and were used in similar ways. The burial chambers were used to store the remains of the dead which were usually de-fleshed and deposited in a disarticulated condition. Tombs may have been re-entered from time to time and the bones removed and circulated as part of an ancestor worship

cult, before being returned to the grave. As many as thirty to forty individuals may have been interred within the chambers and tombs may have remained open for lengthy periods. At the end of their active use the passages were frequently blocked by domestic refuse and the entrance sealed to prevent further access.

Because the chambers take up such a small area of the mound, it has been suggested that the mounds themselves may have been a focus for ritual activities, or that they may have acted as territorial markers. Many Cotswold long barrows have dramatic settings with extensive views, and certainly retain an air of mystery.

Aerial view of Belas Knap long barrow

History

Belas Knap is a particularly fine example of a Neolithic long barrow featuring a false entrance and independently accessible side chambers. Other examples, such as Uley and Nympsfield barrows, have strongly emphasised entrances with chambers opening out on either side of a central passage. At Belas Knap the impressive entrance is a dummy and the burial chambers are entered from the sides of the barrow – when closed and covered by earth they would have been invisible from the outside. It was probably constructed around 3000 BC and would have been used for successive burials over a period of years until eventually the burial chambers were deliberately blocked.

Opinion differs as to the reason for the false portal. It may have been to deter robbers, although little in the way of value has been found in undisturbed tomb chambers. Alternatively, it could be that the false entrance functioned as a 'spirit door', intended to allow the dead to come and go and partake of offerings brought to the tomb by their descendants.

Although Belas Knap seems in good condition, this is the result of several restorations. Romano-British pottery found inside one of the burial chambers show that it was open in Roman times. It was explored between 1863 and 1865 using the archaeological methods of the time, and some years later was restored by Mrs Emma Dent of Sudeley. In 1928–30 the site was excavated again, before being restored as we see it today.

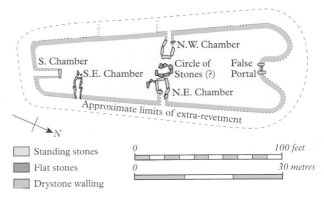

N.W. Chamber
S. Chamber
S.E. Chamber
Circle of Stones (?)
False Portal
N.E. Chamber
Approximate limits of extra-revetment

N

☐ Standing stones
■ Flat stones
☐ Drystone walling

0   100 feet
0   30 metres

Above: *Plan of the barrow*

Left: *A Victorian print showing the false entrance to the north end of the barrow discovered during the 1863–5 excavations*

17

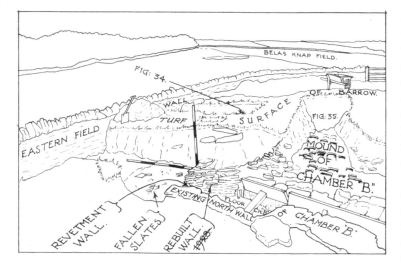

An early 1930s drawing of Belas Knap long barrow

N of

Winchcombe,

½ mile on

Cotswold Way

OS Map 163;

ref SP 021254

Description

Belas Knap long barrow has a trapezoid mound, rather unusually orientated north–south, with a drystone retaining wall. At the northern end of the mound is the forecourt, which consists of a recess flanked by two 'horns', or projections of the mound. This is fronted by the false entrance of two standing stones and a lintel stone. Four burial chambers have been identified within the mound; these

are situated in the south-east, north-east, west and south of the monument. Each chamber was probably enclosed by its own small mound that was later incorporated into the main barrow structure. During the 19th-century excavations, the false entrance was found to cover the remains of six skeletons, including five infants, which are thought to be Early Bronze Age interments. The south-eastern chamber contained the remains of two males and two females along with animal bones and flint artefacts. The north-eastern chamber contained twelve burials, the western chamber fourteen, and the southern chamber just one. The excavators also reported finding a circle of flat stones beneath the centre of the mound, though these were later removed.

History

The Gloucester Blackfriars is one of the most complete Dominican priories to survive from the Middle Ages in England. The mendican orders, or friars, established themselves across Europe in the early 13th century.

They were particularly engaged with preaching and charitable work with the laity. The Dominicans, or Blackfriars, first came to Gloucester in 1239 at the instigation of Sir Stephen de Hermshall. The building of the house began almost immediately,

*Exterior of
Blackfriars priory*

Carved stone lectern at Blackfriars priory

largely with materials and funds donated by Henry III, and was completed in about 1270 as home for some forty friars.

For three centuries the friars were a familiar part of the church establishment, enjoying a revival of popularity at the very end of the Middle Ages. Unfortunately for them, the property they owned was considerable and they were suppressed, along with the larger monasteries, in 1539. By this time the number of friars living in Gloucester had fallen to just six and a prior.

A local alderman called Thomas Bell bought the Gloucester Blackfriars and converted the church into a mansion and the other buildings into a weaving factory. In the 19th century the west range became a row of terraced houses and the library range was used for bottling. Extensive

conservation work has been carried out on the property since it came under guardianship in 1960.

Description

The particular interest of Gloucester's Blackfriars is the complete nature of its survival with several rare features,

Right: Interior of the church nave and north transept looking west

and its history of adaptation and use. The church is on the north side of the quadrangular plan; it is incomplete, for the four arms are all truncated. In the process of conversion, the chancel and nave were reduced and closed off by gable-end walls with central projecting chimney stacks. The north nave aisle was completely demolished while that to the south was partially demolished and the arcades infilled. The chancel became the great hall and floors and partitions were inserted into the former transepts and nave to form chambers. The south transept was subsequently demolished. Since 1960 all post-medieval floors and partitions have been removed to expose the proportions of the church and surviving medieval features.

The magnificent scissor-brace roof is original and documented as a gift from the royal forests during Henry III's reign. The refectory was situated at the south end of the west range and there was a dormitory in the range opposite, above the chapter house where the affairs of the

The first floor of the south range showing the remarkable scissor-brace roof

community were decided. In later years part of this east range became a separate lodging for the prior.

The friars' missionary role meant that the layout of Blackfriars differed in some respects from that of a typical Benedictine or Cistercian abbey. The whole of the upper floor of the south range was occupied by a library that still retains twenty-nine of its original medieval study carrels – a unique survival. The nave of the church was also wider and longer in order to accommodate the large numbers of men and women who came to hear the friars' sermons.

In Blackfriars
Lane, Gloucester
Access only by
guided tour
Tel: 0117 975 0700
OS Map 162;
ref SO 829184

therefore not occupied for long and the army was able to turn its attention to the mineral resources in the Mendips, establishing lead mining – and the attendant silver refining – from the late forties.

During the Roman period, the Bristol, Gloucestershire and Wiltshire region was mostly under the control of a single tribe, the Dobunni. Although precise tribal boundaries are unknown, their territory extended to the north and south, while to the east lay the Atrebates and Belgae. All these tribes were friendly to Rome and did not resist the transit and settlement of the Roman army at the time of the invasion of AD 43. The forts established by the Romans were

Once established, the Romans built new towns and then replaced the largest of the Iron Age settlements in the area. The tribal capital Cirencester, for instance, was located within a few miles of the pre-Roman tribal centre at Bagendon, while the legionary fortress at Gloucester became a colony of veterans at the end of the first century. At Bath, however, the focus was inevitably on the hot spring rather than the Roman fort nearby.

The region flourished under Roman control. Cirencester grew rapidly and soon acquired the major civic buildings seen in any

Above: Reconstruction of Cirencester in the 4th century
Left: Roman statue of a discus thrower

Roman town: the forum, baths and main temple. To these were added town walls and an impressive amphitheatre outside the town. In the countryside, native villages and farmsteads were soon interspersed with villas. Along the roads, small towns grew up, such as Mildenhall, Wiltshire, often meeting a local need for markets, and containing the official staging posts, *mansiones*.

It was during the 3rd and 4th centuries that the region saw really spectacular growth. This was chiefly the result of an administrative reorganisation whereby four new provinces were created out of the old single early province of Britannia. Cirencester, as the capital of the new province Britannia Prima, benefited in particular and its new-found wealth is shown in mosaic workshops catering for the rich and powerful who gravitated to the town to build new houses there. New building is also seen in the countryside and this period witnessed a sharp increase in the number of very large villas such as Great Witcombe. Some of these were developments of earlier farms but others were built

in new locations. The new province quickly established itself and even retained its identity after the Romans abandoned Britain in the 5th century. Thus, in some villas and in the major towns, there is evidence for continued occupation, often with signs of Christian worship, into the 5th or even 6th century. The final demise of this Roman way of life was the Battle of Dyrham, mentioned in the *Anglo-Saxon Chronicle* in AD 577, when 'the kings of Gloucester, Cirencester and Bath' were defeated by the Anglo-Saxon kings of Wessex. Gradually, the Romano-British lifestyle died and was replaced by the new Germanic culture.

Above: Part of a mosaic floor discovered in Cirencester
Left: Roman ring with intaglio

Aerial view of the amphitheatre

History

The Cirencester amphitheatre is one of the largest known examples surviving from the Roman occupation of Britain. It was built just outside the walls of the town (then known as Corinium) early in the 2nd century AD. Cirencester was second only to London in importance at this period with a population of over 10,000 and was at its finest just as Roman rule was collapsing throughout the Western Empire. In AD 408 the last contingents of the regular Roman army left Britain. Without their pay to support the local economy and maintain order, and with no central administration to maintain communications, town life rapidly declined. Private patrons prepared to pay for the public games could not be found. No longer used for the pursuit of pleasure, the amphitheatre became a fortress in an attempt by the town leaders to safeguard their community. Its entrances were narrowed and a ditch dug along the southern sides, and remains of timber buildings dating from the 5th century have also been found. These efforts appear to have been in vain. In AD 577 a stronghold believed to be Cirencester is reported as falling to the advancing Saxons.

The amphitheatre then remained abandoned for several centuries. In the Middle Ages the Abbot of Cirencester enclosed it for use as a rabbit warren. Its local name, the Bull Ring, suggests that it may once have been used for bull-baiting: a return to its original purpose.

Right: An enamelled brooch in the shape of a bird discovered at the site of the amphitheatre

A reconstruction drawing showing how the amphitheatre might have looked in the 2nd century

Description

The amphitheatre is oval in plan (unlike the circular forms built at such places as Dorchester and Silchester), and it has an entrance at each end of the long axis. The massive banks, which are all that can be seen today, supported tiers of seats made from planking on terraced drystone walls. There was also an area for standing spectators and it is estimated that the amphitheatre had a capacity of around 8,000 people. A wall separated the spectators from the arena, which was floored with fine gravel and sand (*harena* being the Latin word for sand).

Of the two entrances, only the eastern one has been excavated. Originally it seems to have been open to the sky, but towards the end of the 2nd century its passageway was vaulted in stone and extra seating was built above it. During the course of a later rebuilding, two small rooms were created on either side of the inner end of the entrance. One may have been used as a shrine to the goddess Nemesis – a common feature of amphitheatres elsewhere in the Roman Empire.

Next to bypass to W of Cirencester. Access from the town or along Chesterton Lane from W end of the bypass, on to Cotswold Ave
OS Map 163; ref SP 020014

The remains of the Roman villa

History

The growth of the new tribal capital of Corinium (Cirencester), the importance of Glevum (Gloucester) and the rich farming land made the Cotswold region a popular area to live during Roman times. The villa at Great Witcombe is one of a group of large houses in the region and was constructed on the steep banks of Birdlip Hill below a line of springs. It was built around AD 250 and there is evidence of two main phases of occupation lasting to the 5th century.

Right: Roman carving of a water spirit

The villa was discovered in 1818 and partially excavated, and there were further excavations in the 20th century.

Description

The villa was terraced and built mainly of the local oolite (limestone), although white marble was imported to make some of the cornices, as well as fine sandstone to provide a suitable surface for painting frescoes. It consisted of two large wings, one of which formed a two- or three-storey residence, with a courtyard. A separate building was connected by a long colonnaded corridor, off which opened a formal reception room. This suite of rooms was used for leisure purposes and was later extended to provide an extra set of baths, set at a lower level and divided from the courtyard by a cross-wall. At about the same time, a large barn-like structure was added to the residential range – again set at a lower level and divided off by a cross-wall.

Left: Reconstruction drawing of how the Roman villa might have looked in its heyday

Below: Drawing of a mosaic pavement found at the villa

This may have reflected a major change of use with the buildings now being used for a cult based on the worship of water and water spirits. A hint of this can be seen in the mosaic pavements preserved under the modern building where fragments of the columns and the villa's hypocaust system can also be seen. Although the views from the villa were spectacular, the slope and the springs caused the foundations to slip and there is evidence that buttresses had to be added to prop up many walls.

5 miles SE of Gloucester off A417; ½ mile S of reservoir in Witcombe Park; 440 yds (400 m) from Cotswold Way National Trail OS Map 163; ref SO 899142 Open: exterior any reasonable time, mosaics by arrangement

View of the remains of the friary church

History

The Grey Friars, or Franciscans, were followers of St Francis of Assisi and founded many religious houses across Europe. They earned their name from the grey habits that were worn as a symbol of their vow of poverty. The Franciscan friary at Gloucester was founded in 1231, but in about 1518 a prominent local family, the Berkeleys of Berkeley Castle, paid for the church to be rebuilt in Perpendicular Gothic style. This incorporated the earlier church but only survived a short while as the friary was surrendered to the king in 1539 at the suppression of the monasteries. Over the following years, the buildings were put to a number of different uses and in 1643 they were severely damaged by Royalist forces during the siege of Gloucester. By 1721 only the nave and its north aisle survived and later in the 18th century houses were built within the walls. In 1810 a large house was built into the west end of the medieval remains and this is now a public library.

Description

The friary would have conformed to the usual monastic plan with a large church and then the chapter house, refectory, dormitory and other buildings ranged round a central cloister. Most have been totally demolished, but the remains of the church can still be seen – its spacious proportions demonstrate that it was designed to hold large congregations in keeping with the Franciscans' mission to the laity and their fame as preachers. The nave and the north aisle still survive and reveal the high quality of the original building. As in many other friaries, the aisle was almost as wide as the nave itself and would originally have had seven bays. The early 19th-century house, which is now the library, occupies the site of the two western bays and has the

remains of the south wall of the nave, and the north wall of the north aisle incorporated into its side walls. In each bay large four-light arched windows can be seen, and at the east end of the north aisle there is evidence of a six-light window. Some of these windows still have portions of Perpendicular tracery. At the south side of the nave there is a trace of the former north walk of the cloister. Reset in the outer face of the south wall of the nave are two stone shields carved with the arms of Chandos and Clifford of Frampton that may originally have decorated a funerary monument. There was also a large cemetery to the north of the church where many of the benefactors of the friary found a resting place.

Above: Detail of the carved decoration below one of the windows

Left: Detail of an arch and windows that still retain portions of tracery

On Greyfriars Walk, Gloucester OS Map 162; ref SO 832184

29

History

In 1149 William of Berkeley, whose family was rising to prominence in Gloucestershire, persuaded Cistercian monks from Tintern Abbey to found a community at Kingswood. The site of the 12th-century abbey is popularly believed to be Abbey Farm, but there is little evidence to support this claim. In about 1149 most of the brothers moved to Hazleton and the abbey was reduced to the status of a grange, the centre of an agricultural estate. In 1164–70, however, the monks returned and founded a new abbey on a more favourable site near the river, and this flourished until its suppression in 1538. It probably followed the normal plan with a church, chapter house, refectory, dormitory and other buildings grouped round a cloister and garth (garden). In Cistercian abbeys there was a separate dormitory for the lay brothers, and other buildings such as the infirmary and guesthouse would have stood in an outer precinct, together with barns and stables.

Description

All that now remains of the abbey is the early 16th-century gatehouse with a range of precinct wall on each side, although there are signs of earthworks in the surrounding fields. It is built of ashlar with a Cotswold stone-tile roof and has two entrances, one for wheeled traffic and the other for pedestrians. A canopied niche over the latter entrance once contained a statue of the Virgin Mary, although all that can now be seen is a dove representing the Holy Spirit. Over the main arch is a mullioned window with the figure of God the Father carved into the tracery and below it is a carving of a pot of lilies. Taken together, the whole composition must represent the Annunciation – an appropriate way to remind those entering the abbey that they were crossing a spiritual as well as a material threshold. The upper room of the gatehouse is reached from a stone doorway immediately to the rear of the gateway.

The gate passage has a lierne vault (ie one with ribs running between bosses as well as to and from the wall).

A 14th-century drawing of a Cistercian monk

Facing page, left: The gatehouse of the Cistercian abbey

In Kingswood off B4060 1 mile SW of Wotton-under-Edge
Exterior open any reasonable time.
Key for interior: 3 Wotton Road, Abbey Street, 10am–3.30pm weekdays
OS Map 162; ref ST 747920

31

Above: Notgrove long barrow in the 1950s

Right: A shale bead excavated from the barrow

History

Built some 5,000 years ago, this Neolithic long barrow forms part of the Cotswold Severn group. It has been excavated twice: by George Witts in 1881 and more extensively by E M Clifford in 1934–5. The earlier excavations revealed that some of the chambers had been previously explored and looted. The stones were grassed over in 1976 to protect them from further deterioration.

Description

Winter is a good time to visit this site as the trees, which have now grown up around the barrow, will have lost their leaves and the position of the barrow on the crest of a high ridge across the Cotswold Hills can be appreciated. Also, the grass, which now covers the site, will be short – it is allowed to grow through the summer months to encourage rare plants. The tomb underneath this grassy mound has to be imagined. Trapezoidal in plan, it is 157 ft (48 m) long, 79 ft (24 m) wide and was once retained by an enclosing double kerb of stone (see plan on p15). The entrance to the barrow faces east and, in front of the mound, was a curved forecourt that would have been used for ceremonies. A central passage leads from the entrance, with two opposing pairs of chambers opening off it with a fifth chamber at the far end. Beyond this, and an unusual feature, was a circular, domed structure covering a stone-lined grave. This appears to be the earliest feature on the site and contained the crouched burial of an adult male. On top of the structure were the bones of a young female. The remains of at least six individuals were found in the passage and chambers, and those of two or more young people beneath the forecourt. There were also teeth and bones from an ox, a dog's tooth, a leaf-shaped flint arrowhead, a black oval bead and

sherds of pottery. These items probably had some ritual significance and, together with the skeletons, are now in Cheltenham Museum.

Grass now covers the stones (below) to protect them

1½ miles NW of
Notgrove on
A436
OS Map 163;
ref SP 096212

History

Nympsfield long barrow stands high on the Cotswold scarp near Frocester with spectacular views over the Severn Valley. Constructed in the Neolithic period, it has long been surrounded by legends and bizarre stories, including one that it was a refuge for lepers. Excavations were carried out by Professor Buckman in 1862, Mrs Clifford in 1937 and in 1974 when the barrow was redisplayed following further work by Alan Saville. The remains of at least thirteen human skeletons as well as Neolithic pottery have been recovered during

Nympsfield long barrow revealing clearly the layout of the burial chambers

excavations. These included a skeleton of a child that was enclosed in a stone cist or coffin in the northern burial chamber. The excavations also found later Neolithic pottery within the blocking of the entrance to the burial chamber, suggesting that the gallery was closed before the end of the Neolithic period.

Description

The barrow is almost oval in plan, measuring 98 ft (30 m) from east to west, 82 ft (25m) from north to south at the western end. The mound was ploughed over and the roof removed at some point in its history, and the chambers remain uncovered today allowing the layout to be seen clearly. The mound is composed of small stones and has a maximum height of around 4 ft (1.2 m).

At the eastern end is a forecourt in the form of a recess flanked by projections of the mound. This leads into an east-facing entrance defined by two standing stones. Beyond the entrance is a stone gallery that leads into a pair of side chambers and an end chamber. The internal chambers were constructed of oolite (limestone), probably quarried nearby. Upright stones line the central passage, with the spaces filled by drystone walling; the barrow was originally surrounded by a drystone kerb, which is now covered over.

Above: The entrance to the barrow

Left: A fragment of Neolithic pottery

1 mile NW of Nympsfield on B4066
OS Map 162;
ref SO 794013

35

ODDA'S CHAPEL

Right: The stone
Anglo-Saxon chapel
attached to a timber-
framed house

Facing page: The
famous Odda Stone
which is now in the
Ashmolean Museum
in Oxford

History

Odda's Chapel at Deerhurst is one
of the most complete surviving
Saxon churches in England. It lay
undiscovered for centuries, its
walls hidden amidst the rambling
rooms of the 17th-century
farmhouse known as Abbot's
Court. The nave had been made
into a kitchen, with a fireplace
and inserted windows, while the
chancel had become a bedroom.

There is evidence of a Roman
villa in the vicinity of the chapel
and Deerhurst was an important
place during the Saxon period.
The present parish church, also a
celebrated Anglo-Saxon survival, is
part of a medieval priory founded
in the 7th century. The existence of
this smaller Saxon chapel nearby was
unknown until 1865 when the Revd
George Butterworth rediscovered it.
Two clues helped him. The first was
an entry in the medieval chronicle of
Tewkesbury Abbey describing a church
dedicated to the Holy Trinity that stood
opposite the gateway to Deerhurst

Priory. The second was the famous
Odda Stone that had been found in
an orchard near the parish church in
1675. The inscription on it stated:

*'Earl Odda had this Royal Hall built
and dedicated in honour of the Holy
Trinity for the soul of his brother Aelfric,
which left the body in this place. Bishop*

Ealdred dedicated it the second of the Ides of April in the fourteenth year of the reign of Edward, King of the English.'

Earl Odda was related to Edward the Confessor and, for a short time, was responsible for the government of an extensive area of south-west England. His brother, Aelfric, in whose memory the building was erected, had died in Deerhurst three years earlier. Edward the Confessor conveyed the chapel, along with the Manor of Deerhurst, to the Abbey of Westminster shortly before his death. The chapel probably went out of use in the 13th century.

Description

The chapel comprises a square-ended chancel divided from the nave by a solid chancel arch. The main Saxon features are the alternating long and short quoins, the windows, the chancel arch and the north door of the nave. The nave walls are 17 ft (5.2 m) high and are built of local blue lias stone. There were originally

two doorways facing each other but the one on the south side has been blocked. The window on the south side is near perfect, even containing some of the original oak framework. Traces of the fireplace of the later Tudor kitchen can be seen in the west wall. The chancel arch is just over 10 ft (3 m) high and slightly horseshoe-shaped. The chancel beyond has been extensively altered. The south wall was demolished and its position is now marked by the low wall. The upper storey was inserted when the building was converted into part of the adjoining dwelling.

In Deerhurst off B4213 at Abbot's Court, SW of church Open: 1 Apr–31 Oct: 10am–6pm daily. 1 Nov–31 Mar: 10am–4pm daily Closed 24–26 Dec and 1 Jan *OS Map 150; ref SO 869298*

Above: The great bank of the section of Offa's Dyke in English Heritage guardianship

Right: A silver penny minted in the reign of Offa, King of Mercia

History

Offa was the King of the Mercians, a warrior tribe from central England, from 747 to 796 AD. He had seized power during a time of great unrest caused by friction between Wales and England in the border region. Offa was determined to quell the unruly Welsh and impose his authority and this he did by building one of the most remarkable structures in Britain. Sometime during the 780s, Offa decided on the construction of a great earth-wall and ditch, or dyke, running from 'sea to sea'. The work required thousands of men, and each section seems to have been built by people from a different district. The fact that this mammoth undertaking was achieved illustrates the cohesion of the kingdom at this time. The dyke was never garrisoned but would have been manned by relatively small local forces.

Offa died in 796 in a battle against the Welsh: it is believed that he was trying to establish a final link in the dyke to the Irish Sea in the north. After his death his kingdom gradually declined until it was completely crushed by the Viking invasion. The border area, however, remained crucial in British history.

Description

Offa's Dyke covers 82 miles (132 km) of the total distance of 149 miles (240 km) between Prestatyn in the north to Sedbury in the south, the intervening gaps being filled by natural features such as slopes and rivers. It consists of an earth bank, which in places still stands to a height of 12 ft (3.5 m), fronted by a deep quarry-ditch with a total width of up to 60 ft (18 m). Excavation has confirmed that a wooden breastwork ran along the top of the bank, and in places this was later rebuilt in stone. The west side of the bank was also revetted with turf to create a near vertical face. Possibly some sort of palisade or wall also existed. It is thought that towers may have been erected at intervals, though none has yet been found. In places it runs absolutely straight for miles – proof of the technical skills of its engineers.

Left: Admiring the view of Tintern Abbey from the Devil's Pulpit

Located 3 miles NE of Chepstow off B4228. Access via Forest Enterprise Tidenham car park, 1 mile walk down to The Devil's Pulpit. Access unsuitable for the very young, old or infirm. Proper walking shoes are necessary. *OS Map 162; ref SO 516011- ST 549975*

History

The first recorded bridge at Over is mentioned in the Domesday Book in 1089. It was situated at a convenient crossing point over the River Severn for routes running west out of Gloucester, spanning what is locally known as the Maisemore Channel. The bridge was a county responsibility, meaning that it was maintained by rates levied for the purpose – a system that had its origins in Saxon times.

In 1825 Thomas Telford (1757-1834), one of Britain's greatest engineers, designed a new bridge to replace a Tudor one that had been damaged by ice in 1818, and whose narrow arches had restricted river traffic. He supplied two designs for the bridge – one of cast iron, similar to one he designed to cross the River Severn at Mythe, near Tewkesbury, and the other of stone based on the 18th-century bridge across the River

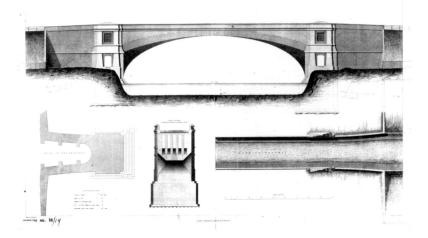

A 19th-century plan of Over Bridge

Seine at Neuilly, built by the French architect Perronet.

The new bridge, built to the second design, was opened in 1830. It was the lowest practicable crossing point of the river – before the great Severn Suspension Bridge was built at Aust in the 1960s. In spite of the early subsidence, the bridge withstood the increasing volume of heavy traffic passing over it until the early 1960s, when the present dual carriage and new steel bridge were built to the north.

Description

Over Bridge is a single-span arch bridge approximately 328 ft (100 m) long and 30 ft (9 m) wide. It was constructed about 295 ft (90 m) upstream from the previous bridge, requiring major changes to the approach roads. Telford employed the 'cornes de vache' technique whereby horn shapes are cut out of the sides of the bridge with the aim of reducing

the turbulence and increasing the flow of water in times of flood. The technique also gives the illusion of a longer, flatter arch. Construction of the bridge involved the use of a curved wooden support system, called 'centring', to hold up the wedge-shaped stones that formed the arch. Unfortunately, when the centring was removed on the bridge's completion, the settlement of soft ground around the bridge caused the crown of the arch to drop by 10 inches (25 cm). This movement did not affect its strength.

Telford's elegant stone bridge spanning the River Severn

I mile NW of Gloucester city centre at junction of A40 (Ross) and A417 (Ledbury)
OS Map 162;
ref SO 816196

The impressive gatehouse to the castle

History

St Briavel's was an important royal castle on the frontier with Wales and the administrative and judicial centre of the Forest of Dean. Built in the early 12th century, it was the residence of the warden of the Forest of Dean – a royal hunting ground where the game was protected and the king alone allowed to hunt. The castle was in royal possession by the 1160s and was rebuilt, with the small but impressive keep, by Henry II (1154–89). The Forest of Dean was important for another reason – it was one of the centres of the medieval iron industry, small scale by present day standards but a vital source of supply for the manufacture of weapons, especially crossbow bolts. The crossbow was the favourite weapon of the mercenaries who were employed in considerable numbers by Henry's son, King John (1199–1216), who built a new hall (now vanished) and an elaborate chamber block at St Briavel's.

In spite of this, John only visited St Briavel's five times in the course of seventeen years, staying no more than eleven days altogether. John's son, Henry III, also visited the castle from time to time, adding a small chapel to his father's house. By this time the castle was functioning more as an administrative headquarters and workshop than a stronghold.

Under Edward I (1272–1307), thousands of crossbow bolts were produced at the castle in preparation for the king's Welsh and Scottish campaigns. Edward took care to ensure that his arsenal was well protected, adding the massive twin-towered gatehouse to the castle in 1292. With the conquest of Wales completed by the end of the 15th century, the castle's importance declined rapidly and unused buildings were demolished in 1680. The gatehouse became a prison where those accused of committing offences within the forest area were held while awaiting trial. A number of prisoners' inscriptions remain which testify to the unwholesomeness of the gaol but the legend that criminals were hanged from the battlements seems unlikely. Fines were a far more profitable form of punishment – or mutilation, which served as a public reminder of the consequences of breaking the King's law. The keep collapsed in 1752, by which time the great hall had also been demolished, and the east tower collapsed in 1777 destroying the adjoining buildings. The castle was

A reconstruction bird's eye view of the castle

still being used as a debtors' prison until 1842.

After centuries of neglect and decay, the surviving buildings were restored and rendered habitable at the turn of the 20th century. Today St Briavel's enjoys a peaceful life as a youth hostel with visitors sleeping in the gatehouse prison.

43

Plan of St Briavel's Castle

Description

The castle is situated on the edge of a steep scarp above the River Wye. Its irregular plan has led to the suggestion that it lies on the site of an earlier earthwork – perhaps a Norman 'motte and bailey' arrangement. By the later 12th century, a square stone keep, said to have been over 100 ft (30 m) high, was built on top of the castle motte and in the 13th century a curtain wall was added, enclosing an area of 1½ acres (0.61 ha).

Other alterations included the construction of a two-storey domestic range, thought to have been the 'royal apartments' mentioned in documents of 1227. A twin-towered gatehouse with a defended passage was also added and this, in turn, was replaced with the existing gatehouse by Edward I in 1292–3 to improve the defences against Welsh attack. It was designed as a 'keep gatehouse' – a gatehouse that could be closed and defended against attack from the rear as well as the front. There were three sets of portcullises that turned

the entrance passage into a lethal 'killing ground'.

The castle's surviving fabric dates mainly from the 13th century and consists of a dry moat, curtain walls, fragments of the keep, a two-storey domestic range and chapel, the site of the hall, and the twin-towered gatehouse with defended passage and rooms over it.

In St Briavel's, 7 miles NE of Chepstow off B4228
Exterior open any reasonable time
Bailey: 1 Apr–30 Sept: 1pm–4pm daily
OS Map 162; ref SO 559046

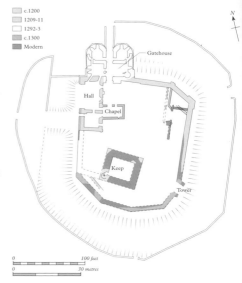

c.1200
1209-11
1292-3
c.1300
Modern

Gatehouse
Hall
Chapel
Keep
Tower
N
0   100 feet
0   30 metres

St Mary's, Kempley

History

Nine hundred years ago, the manor of Kempley belonged to one of the most powerful men in England – Baron Hugh de Lacy of Longtown Castle, near Hereford, the trusted counsellor of Henry I (1100–35). It was probably Hugh de Lacy who built Kempley church, perhaps commissioning the remarkable paintings in the chancel as a memorial to his father, Walter de Lacy, a Norman baron and veteran of the Battle of Hastings.

The large west tower of the church was built during the 13th century, when the Welsh wars of Edward I exposed Kempley to reprisal raids, although there are no records of the church being attacked. Instead it became steadily more isolated as the villagers of Kempley moved to higher ground two miles away.

Above: The timber-framed church porch

Right: Medieval wall paintings under the chancel arch

In the 16th century, when images in churches had to be removed following the Reformation, the paintings were covered over with whitewash. They were rediscovered in the 20th century, and have now been cleaned and conserved.

Description

The church consists of a stone-built chancel and nave with a timber-framed south porch and a squat west tower. Much of the fabric dates from the 12th century, with the tower added in the 13th century. The survival of a set of early 12th-century wall paintings within a church of about the same date is unusual. Even more extraordinary is the fact that the roof timbers also date from this period.

The subject of the paintings in the chancel seems to be the Last Judgement. In the centre of the barrel-vaulted ceiling Christ sits upon a rainbow, adored by winged angels (seraphim); on either side of him stand the twelve apostles, with the Virgin Mary and St Peter closest to the chancel arch. Above the simple round-headed windows there are representations of the heavenly Jerusalem, and between the windows and the east wall there are two figures with the hats and staffs of lay pilgrims. These are almost certainly

Hugh and Walter de Lacy. The identity of the bishops painted on either side of the east window is not known, but they may be early popes.

Wall paintings of this kind are very rare in England and their muted colours and treatment of drapery are typical of the Romanesque style of painting in France. The artist may well have been a French monk from Hugh de Lacy's own foundation at Llanthony Priory.

In the nave of the church there are more paintings of a slightly later, probably 14th-century, date. These are worked in tempera painted on dry lime mortar unlike those in the chancel which are frescoes (painted directly onto wet plaster). Their subjects – appropriate for the nave of a church, which was used by the laity – warn of the dangers of temptation; they include the Wheel of Life and St Anthony and the Devil.

Below: Painting of the Wheel of Life in the nave of the church. The window recess to the right is decorated with figures of St Anthony on one side and St Michael and the Virgin Mary

1 mile N of Kempley off B4024, 6 miles NE of Ross-on-Wye Open: 1 Mar–31 Oct: 10am–6pm daily; Winter opening by appointment Tel: 01531 660214 OS Map 149; ref SO 670313

Above: The fine long barrow at Uley

Below: Neolithic flint scrapers found near Uley

3½ miles NE of Dursley on B4066
OS Map 162; ref SO 790000

History

Uley Long Barrow (known locally as Hetty Pegler's Tump after Hester Pegler who owned the land in the 17th century) is a Neolithic burial mound, at least 5,000 years old and impressively sited overlooking the Severn Valley. Between fifteen and twenty skeletons have been recovered from the mound over the years but we know little about the subsequent history of these finds. Two skulls went to Guy's Hospital in London, but it is said that most of the bones were reburied in Uley churchyard.

Despite its apparently good condition, Uley Barrow has suffered considerably from vandalism and casual excavation. Coins and pieces of broken pot found inside the barrow indicate that it was opened in Roman times. It was probably broken into again in the Middle Ages and damaged further in the 19th century. The barrow as seen today is largely the result of the excavation and reconstruction undertaken by Dr John Thurnham in 1854 and subsequent repairs in 1871, 1891 and 1906.

Description

The barrow is 120 ft (37 m) long and 10 ft (3 m) wide and of the 'transepted' type: its cruciform plan resembles that of a church with two pairs of chambers opening out of a central passage. The central passageway leads to an end chamber and two side chambers on the left or south side. The north passage wall is a conjectural reconstruction but is known to have fronted two matching northern chambers, one of which was destroyed in 1821 by workmen seeking stone. It is one of the best surviving of the Cotswold Severn group – and one of the most atmospheric.

History

This barrow, also known as Rodmarton long barrow, is of early Neolithic date (c4000–3500 BC). It seems that the site was used for burials well after the Neolithic period as Roman pottery and coins of Claudius Gothicus (AD 168–70) have been found. The barrow was excavated in the late 19th century, and also in 1939 when thirteen skeletons were found as well as leaf-shaped arrowheads. When two trees fell down in the great storms of 1987 they revealed a previously unknown chamber situated to the south-west of the north chamber. A large capstone and the bones of a child were also discovered.

Description

Set on a gentle slope immediately below the crest of a ridge, the chambered long barrow is trapezoidal in plan and measures 187 ft (57 m) by 89 ft (27 m). The mound is made up of small stones to a height of 9 ft (2.75 m) and was originally flanked by ditches where the material to construct the barrow had been quarried. At the eastern end of the mound there is a forecourt flanked by two projections and a so-called false entrance consisting of two standing stones and a stone lintel, blocked by a slab. This entrance seems to have been constructed at the same time as the forecourt with which it is associated but it does not provide any access into the monument. There are at least three stone-lined chambers and the northern one was where the skeletons were discovered. The southern chamber is approached by an entrance from the side of the mound via a short passage. Animal bones and human remains have been recovered from this chamber. The barrow is a fine example of the Cotswold Severn type.

The remains of the Cotswold Severn barrow at Rodmarton

I mile SW of Rodmarton
OS Map 163;
ref ST 933973

The region has a rich legacy of art and literature. Amongst Bristol's artistic progeny are a precocious poet, a 'Blue Stocking' writer and a 'land artist'. Thomas Chatterton, born in 1752, claimed to have discovered medieval manuscripts in St Mary Redcliffe church, and his subsequent exposure as their forger may have led to his suicide in 1770. His contemporary, playwright and essayist Hannah More, was born at Fishponds in 1745, and spent her secluded later years at Cowslip Green, near Bristol. The work of artist Richard Long, born in 1945, treats his country walks as art works, revealing his relationship with the local landscape. The only artist to be shortlisted for the Turner prize four times up to now, his *White Water Line* won the prize in 1989.

The counties of Wiltshire and Gloucestershire have many associations with great English poets. The metaphysical poet, George Herbert (1593–1633), was rector of Bemerton from 1630. His major work, *The Temple*, was published shortly after his death. Herbert was a great influence on Siegfried Sassoon's later work, though Sassoon is best known for his early poetry, such as *Counter Attack*, 1918. Sassoon attended Marlborough College and returned to Wiltshire in 1932 where he spent the last 35 years of his life quietly at Heytesbury House.

The artist John Constable, though Suffolk-born, also celebrated the Wiltshire countryside. It was Stonehenge, and especially

Above: The Suicide of Thomas Chatterton *by Henry Wallis, 1856*
Left: *The writer Richard Jefferies*

Salisbury Cathedral, that provided the inspiration for some of his most remarkable paintings.

Richard Jefferies, one of England's most individual writers on the countryside, was born in 1848 at Coate, Swindon, in the house that is now a museum to him. His great love of nature comes across vividly in novels such as *Wood Magic* (1881). A commemorative sarsen stone inscribed with words from Jefferies' autobiography, *The Story of my Heart* (1883), stands at Burderop Down: 'It is Eternity now, I am in the midst of it. It is about me in the sunshine.'

Born at Slad in the Cotswolds in 1914, Laurie Lee famously recreated his boyhood in the first of three autobiographical volumes: *Cider with Rosie* (1959). Playwright Dennis Potter, born in a coal miner's cottage in the Forest of Dean, portrayed his own vision of childhood in his 1979 play *Blue Remembered Hills*.

Children's writer Beatrix Potter based *The Tailor of Gloucester* (1902) on stories she heard while visiting cousins at Harescombe Grange

near Stroud. An earlier tailor of Gloucester was the father of First World War poet Ivor Gurney. Born in the city in 1890, Gurney continued to write poems evoking his beloved Gloucestershire until his death in 1937. Writer Edward Thomas brought his love of the English countryside into his war poems, and in Adlestrop he immortalised the Gloucestershire village, recalling a moment when his train paused at its quiet station and he heard 'all the birds of Oxfordshire and Gloucestershire'.

Above: Stonehenge *by John Constable, 1836*

Left: *Illustration from* The Tailor of Gloucester *by Beatrix Potter*

WILTSHIRE

Unstaffed sites
Staffed sites

Windmill Hill
Avebury Stone Circles
West Kennet Avenue & Long Barrow
Alexander Keiller Museum
Silbury Hill
Bradford-on-Avon Tithe Barn
The Sanctuary
Chisbury Chapel
Hatfield Earthworks
Bratton Camp & White Horse
Ludgershall Castle & Cross
Netheravon Dovecote
Stonehenge
Woodhenge
Old Sarum
Old Wardour Castle

Wiltshire is typified by the vast expanses of chalk downs that form one of the richest archaeological landscapes in the world. Once part of the great Saxon Kingdom of Wessex, its ancient towns and villages are full of historical interest. The mighty prehistoric earthworks of Old Sarum became one of the most prominent places in the medieval realm with a royal castle and cathedral. A new cathedral was built in nearby Salisbury in the 13th century and its soaring spire is the tallest in England.

Above: 'The Manger' below Uffington Castle and White Horse

Right: Salisbury Cathedral

The wool trade brought wealth to the largely pastoral agricultural community but the industrial revolution and the advent of the railways led to the growth of Swindon as a railway, industrial and commercial centre.

The Downs above West Kennet

Western portal of Twerton Tunnel near Bath

in 1841 with the completion of the Box Tunnel, the greatest engineering feat of the early railway age. Built to Brunel's broad gauge of seven feet, the Great Western's works achieved a grandeur unmatched elsewhere in the country and, as they were especially suited to high speed, most of its structures have survived in daily use with the section from Wiltshire to Bristol running on largely unaltered formations.

The Great Western Railway is very much a railway of two parts – Brunel's 'billiards table' to the east of Swindon and the stretch to the west where he concentrated all his main gradients. These two sections of the railway sit very differently in their respective landscapes reflecting not only the different topography and local building materials but above all Brunel's sense of place and drama. Thus to the east of Swindon the rivers with their wide, gentle valleys are spanned by gracious, rather austere, brick structures, while to the west the hills are pierced by tunnels with highly embellished portals and rivers crossed by appropriately dramatic bridges. The features on the section through Wiltshire and on to Bath and

The Great Western Railway between London and Bristol was authorised by Parliament in 1835 and the detail of its design and construction was entirely the conception of Isambard Kingdom Brunel. According to Brunel it was to be 'the finest work in England' and it opened throughout

The 'Arches', Chippenham, as depicted by J C Bourne (1846)

of the incline at Wootton Bassett to the west no longer present the obstacle to locomotives that they once did, but the embankment through Chippenham still divides the town and is pierced by handsome monumental arches.

The railway drops down through the Cotswold escarpment by means of the Box Tunnel, 3,195 yards (2,922 m) long. Its massive, classically detailed, western portal and the more refined and equally elegant portals of Middle Hill tunnel, announce the

Chippenham Viaduct – the 'Arches' today

Bristol comprise an unfolding essay in architectural styles and are best experienced, as Brunel intended, from the landscapes through which the railway passes.

The journey begins at Swindon where Brunel, on the advice of his gifted mechanical engineer Daniel Gooch, sited his main engineering works close to the only junction station on the original line. Swindon Station has lost its grandeur but the Works and Railway Village, now adapted and restored, comprise the finest surviving example in the world of an early railway engineering works with its planned settlement. The cuttings and embankments

Brunel's Train Shed, Temple Meads Station (J C Bourne, 1846) – now the function room of the British Empire and Commonwealth Museum

railway's arrival in the Avon valley. The classical theme is maintained on the approaches to Bath with the graceful bridges at Bathford and, in the city itself, the handsome landscaped section through Sydney Gardens and St James Bridge over the Avon.

At Bath Spa Station the architecture changes abruptly to echo earlier historical styles. From here to Bristol, styles vary from Jacobean to medieval with the turreted bridge and viaduct to the west of

Sydney Gardens, Bath – the most gracious railway urban landscape in the country

the station, the castellated portals of Twerton and Fox Hill tunnels and the gothic-arched bridge spanning the Avon in Bristol. The magnificent Bristol Temple Meads terminus with its mock hammer-beam train shed fronted by offices and boardroom behind a 'Tudorbethan' baronial façade announced the railway's arrival in Bristol.

Today, the spirit of Brunel is everywhere to be seen along the route of the Great Western, emphasising now, just as it did a century and a half ago, that to travel by train is not just a journey from here to there but an experience to be relished.

The GWR cutting through Sydney Gardens and Bathwick Hill in Bath with the Kennet and Avon Canal alongside

History

The Avebury complex is one of the principal ceremonial sites of Neolithic Britain that we can visit today. It was built and altered over many centuries from about 2850 BC until around 2200 BC and is one of the largest, and undoubtedly the most complex, surviving Neolithic henge monument in Britain.

The exact sequence of construction of the banks, ditches (called henges) and stone circles is still not completely understood. Limited excavations and more recent aerial and geophysical surveys indicate that many other features once existed within the enclosure, and it is quite likely that, before the stone circles were erected, timber circles and structures may have originally filled the area within the bank – as at other henges in this part of Britain.

At some stage, two avenues of stones were also built, linking the Great Henge with other ceremonial sites at Beckhampton and Overton Hill. The huge man-made mound of Silbury Hill stands not far away and is also broadly contemporary with these monuments. The impression gained is of a landscape being shaped for rituals that involved inclusion, exclusion and procession. If this is correct, then the various monuments may have been built as public 'theatres' for rites and ceremonies that gave physical expression to the community's ideas of world order; the place of the people within that order; the relationship between the people and their gods; and the nature and

Aerial view of Avebury

transmission of authority (whether spiritual or political). The length of time over which the Great Henge and its two avenues were built is so long that it suggests the community's understanding of its environment may gradually have altered – and that changing rituals may have been the driving force for the building of new monuments and for their eventual abandonment around 1800 BC.

Description

As the site appears now, it consists of a huge circular bank and ditch with four causewayed entrances and an inner circle of upright stones enclosing a further two stone circles, each with a central feature. A double avenue of stones leads away from the southern entrance towards the Sanctuary stone circles on Overton Hill, about a mile (1.6 km) to the south east.

The massive bank and ditch enclose an area of 28.5 acres (11.5 ha). The shape formed by the ditch is sub-circular and is divided by

causewayed entrances into four unequal arcs. The bank is now some 14–18 ft (4.2–5.4 m) high but was once nearly 55 ft (17 m) above what was originally a 30 ft (9 m) deep ditch. The bank of stark white chalk must have been a spectacular sight.

A reconstruction painting of how Avebury might have looked in the Neolithic period

Skeleton excavated from the site

with Stonehenge and Silbury Hill.

There are three great stone circles within the henge at Avebury: an outer circle and two smaller inner circles that were aligned more or less north and south. The main outer circle probably had between 98 and 105 stones arranged around the perimeter edge of the surrounding ditch.

It is as irregular as the ditch in shape and appears to have been built by different work gangs. Where the bank ended at an entrance, timber revetments appear to have been used to keep the bank in place. The surfaces of the four causewayed entrances were reduced by scraping the top layer of chalk, so that the banks each side appeared even higher and more impressive. There may also have been timber entrances of some kind, restricting access to the circles to only a few people at a time. Together with the stones, the Great Henge at Avebury took many hundreds of thousands of hours to complete. It was one of the most labour-intensive Neolithic monuments in Britain along

Right: How the sarsen stones may have been placed in position

The stones were quite variable in shape and size, but the tallest ones stood at the northern and southern entrances to the henge – presumably placed to form impressive openings. The southern circle focused on a central point, the great Obelisk, which was the largest stone in the circle at 21 ft (6.4 m) high. This was removed sometime after 1725 and its former position is now represented by a concrete post. It was surrounded by twenty-nine smaller stones, which formed the circle. These were set at regular intervals, about 36 ft (11 m)

apart, the same as the stones in the outer circles and also of roughly the same height. Around the central point of the Obelisk, an arrangement of smaller rough sarsen stones formed a near rectangular enclosure that had already been staked out with wooden posts. When excavated this curious alignment was called the 'Z' feature. South of it was a single stone, perhaps lining up with the southern causewayed entrance.

The northern circle probably consisted of twenty-seven stones, also spaced at the interval used elsewhere at Avebury of about 36 ft (11 m). Most of the original stones are now missing, but two still stand and two more lie on the ground. At the centre are the remains of the Cove, or the Devil's Brandirons, as it was known. This once consisted of three rectangular shaped sarsen stones, arranged around three sides of a square with the opening to the north. Although not visible today, it is likely that, like the Obelisk in the southern

Some of the standing stones at Avebury

Left: Part of the stone circle

An 18th-century drawing of Avebury

7 miles W of
Marlborough
Visitor car park
(free to EH
members) is S
of Avebury off
the A4361. Free
disabled parking
in village car
park only
OS Map 173;
ref SU 102700

circle, the Cove was surrounded by rows or a ring of smaller sarsen stones.

In the Middle Ages the stones may have been associated with pagan and devil worship and many were either buried or destroyed. Later building and agricultural improvements led to others being removed. Records and maps made by early antiquarians such as John Aubrey and William Stukeley give us some clues as to its former layout. The appearance of the site today, however, owes much to Alexander Keiller, heir to a fortune made from the famous Keiller marmalade, who bought the site and cleared away buildings and re-erected many stones in the late 1930s. Today, Avebury (along with Stonehenge) is designated a World Heritage Site.

A reconstruction drawing showing how part of the Avebury complex might have been used

History

This is one of the country's finest examples of medieval monastic barns – rightly called 'the

Bradford-on-Avon tithe barn was once owned by the richest nunnery in England

cathedrals of the land'. Built in the early years of the 14th century, it originally formed part of a range of farm buildings grouped around an open rectangular yard. Strictly speaking it is not a tithe barn at all but part of a grange. Granges were established so that monastic

establishments could administer their far-flung estates. The owner of the Bradford-on-Avon grange was Shaftesbury Abbey which was the richest nunnery in England and the guardian of the relics of Edward the Martyr (reigned 975–9). The produce of the surrounding estate was brought across the nearby pack-horse bridge to be stored in the great barn before being sold or used by the nuns themselves. When the abbey was dissolved in 1539, the domestic buildings of the Bradford grange became a farm; the barn remaining in use until 1974.

Description

The barn measures 168 ft (51 m) long, spans 33 ft (10 m) and is divided into fourteen large bays. The stunning raised cruck roof is divided by massive 'A' shaped trusses, braced underneath to form point arches. These trusses are joined together lengthwise by purlins which in turn support the rafters and the 100 tons of stone roof tiles. On the north side are two large porches, paired with two smaller ones on the south. Between the porches are threshing floors, set so that dust and chaff would blow out through the open doors. The masonry is of very fine quality throughout and resembles other barns of the same period at Glastonbury, Avebury and Abbotsbury. The numerous masons' marks on the face of many of the stones are worthy of note. Each mason would incise his own mark to ensure that he received the appropriate payment for his work.

There are pairs of porches either side of the barn

Left: *The massive raised cruck roof*

¼ mile S of town centre off B3109
Open: 10.30am–4pm daily
Closed 25 Dec
OS Map 173; ref ST 823604

65

History

Bratton Camp (also known as Bratton Castle) is an Iron Age hillfort, occupied between *c* 300 BC and the time of the Roman invasion in AD 43. It additionally encloses a Neolithic long barrow and adjoins the site of the famous Westbury White Horse on the hillside below. The barrow may have served as a shrine as well as an ancestral tomb providing a focal point for ceremonies in which the dead could act as intermediaries between the living community and the gods.

The Westbury White Horse or the 'old grey mare'

At least 2,000 years separate the long barrow from the Iron Age tribe who built the great earth banks that now surround it. The interior of the hillfort is likely to have been occupied in a similar way to other contemporary hill-top camps in the area with 'streets' of round or oval houses, raised rectangular granaries, temples and evidence of metal working and pottery manufacture. By this time the scattered clans of the earliest times had evolved into a complex society of warring tribes living in what has been described as a kind of 'cattle-rustling wild west'. In this society, the construction of a powerful defence system became the highly visible symbol of each community's status.

Description

The Neolithic long barrow is situated near the centre of the hillfort and, before the building of the fort, would have been clearly visible from all sides. Near the southern entrance of the hillfort is a Bronze Age bowl barrow indicating the continuance of a burial tradition in this place. The hillfort defences take advantage of the steep natural slopes of the chalk escarpment. On the level ground of the plateau the bank and ditch defences are doubled and the fort's entrance is further protected by an outwork or barbican. Originally, the chalk ramparts may have been faced with timber to give a steep outer face topped by a breastwork, while the entrances might have been defended by timber gate towers. The smooth grassy slopes give little idea of just how formidable the hillfort must have been.

The Westbury White Horse is the oldest of the Wiltshire horses. It is also one of the best situated, being high on a very steep slope and overlooking a panoramic view. There has been a white horse on the site for at least 300 years – the earliest mention of it is in 1742. Some believe that the original horse was cut to commemorate the battle of Ethandun, in which King Alfred fought off Viking invaders, and that it looked similar to the white

Aerial view of Bratton Camp and White Horse

horse at Uffington. Today's horse was cut in 1778 by George Gee, steward to Lord Abingdon, who apparently felt that the older version was not a sufficiently good representation of a horse! In the 1950s it was decided that the horse could be more easily maintained if it were set in concrete and painted white. The horse became so discoloured, due to lichen and environmental deposits, that it became known locally as the 'old grey mare'. English Heritage steam-cleaned the horse in 2001.

2 miles E of Westbury off B 3098, 1 mile SW of Bratton OS Map 184; ref ST 900516

67

WILTSHIRE **CHISBURY CHAPEL**

The medieval chapel at Chisbury

History

The Chapel of St Martin is an appealing medieval thatched building, used for over two centuries as a barn. It was built in the second quarter of the 13th century, but incorporates re-used 12th-century stone in its construction which suggests that there may have been an earlier chapel on the site or nearby. It has been interpreted as either the chapel of ease to the parish church of Great Bedwyn, or a free

chapel of the Hampshire abbey of St Denys. It had a resident priest until 1539 and retained an ecclesiastical function until the end of the 17th century. Having fallen into disuse, it became an animal shelter. By the early 20th century, the structure of the chapel was causing concern, and a report of 1938 described its condition as poor, with the timbers of the roof in danger of collapse. Since that time the roof and the stonework have been repaired.

Description

Built of flint with stone quoins, the chapel is 58 ft (17.7 m) long and nearly 26 ft (8 m) wide. It comprises a chancel and nave, formerly divided by a timber rood screen, the ghost outline of which can be seen in the remains of the wall plaster. Above the screen there would have been a rood beam and the sockets of this can still be seen in the walls.

The chapel has very fine windows. These are more numerous and elaborate in the chancel with foliated capitals on truncated shafts, while those in the nave are lancets with cusped heads. The medieval liturgical arrangements can still be made out. Traces of the high altar can be found in the chancel in front of the east window, and there were possibly two smaller altars in the nave, either side of the doorway in the centre of the screen. The truss above the rood is medieval, though the trusses with moulded wall-posts to the west are 17th-century replacements.

The flint walls of the chapel would have been plastered internally and externally and some of this finish can still be seen. Incised on the internal wall plaster, the consecration crosses survive, the best preserved example being on the west wall. The chapel probably always had a thatched roof and this has been renewed a number of times, though some of the original timbers remain.

Left: A lancet window in the chapel

On unclassified road, ¼ mile E of Chisbury, off A1. Situated behind Manor Farm.
OS Map 174; ref SU 280660

The bank and ditch structure of Hatfield Earthworks

History

Hatfield Earthworks consist of a large, irregular-shaped henge enclosure, formed on three sides by a substantial ditch and outer bank and on the other by a loop in the River Avon, within which lie a Neolithic henge and the remains of a monumental mound. It was built in the later Neolithic period, around 2400 BC. The mound was excavated by the famous archaeologist Sir Richard Colt Hoare and his assistant William Cunnington in 1807 but they were disappointed to find no evidence of a burial and the barrow, apparently constructed mainly of sand, fell apart as they dug. These monumental mounds, of which Silbury Hill is the best known example, are exceptionally rare and seem to have had a ceremonial function.

Further excavation in the late 1960s around the north entrance of the enclosure produced quantities of late Neolithic pottery, flints and animal bones, as well as the crouched burial of a young adult female. Evidence of further Neolithic activity was also discovered within the enclosure, including a round timber structure. Only a small area of the enclosure at Hatfield is under English Heritage protection. On this part of the site the bank and ditch structure is particularly clear and there is a good view of the Alton Barnes White Horse.

Description

The area enclosed measures up to 578 yds (530 m) from north to south and 392 yds (360 m) from east to west. There were two entrances, on the north and east sides, but the effects of centuries of erosion and cultivation have made it difficult to see them clearly today. The earthworks appear to have been constructed in short, straight sections and the profile of the ditch and bank varies considerably. In the best preserved section, within woodland, the bank is up to 130 ft (40 m) wide and 9 ft (2.75 m) high.

Inside the enclosure, close to the river, is a small earthwork consisting of a gently domed circular area of 130 ft (40 m) in diameter, surrounded by a ditch approximately 26 ft (8 m) wide and, beyond that, a low bank of 33–39 ft (10–12 m) in width. Immediately inside the eastern entrance lies all that remains of Hatfield Barrow, once an immense monumental mound which, it was claimed, was over 200 ft (70 m) in diameter and more than 30 ft (9 m) high. The ditch from which the material was dug to construct the mound has now been silted up but has been discovered by geophysical survey. As the monument is sited close to the river's source, it has been suggested that there may have been communication between Hatfield and the great henge at Durrington Walls.

Portrait of Sir Richard Colt Hoare

5½ miles SE of Devizes, off A342, NE of Marden village
OS Map 173;
ref SU 092583

Monument on Chatterton Down recording the place where a highway robber died in 1839

Wiltshire abounds with famous archaeological sites, monuments and landscapes, among them the World Heritage Sites of Avebury and Stonehenge. Although these and many others are well known, the most extensive archaeological landscape in this area, that of the Salisbury Plain, is less so. Much of the Plain cannot be accessed as it is owned by the Ministry of Defence and forms the largest army training estate in the UK, but some parts can be visited. The army first bought parts of the Plain in 1897, and the Salisbury Plain Training Area now covers an area about the size of the Isle of Wight – about 9 per cent of the county of Wiltshire. The Plain stretches some 24 miles (38 km) in length from west Hampshire in the east, to the River Wylie in the west, and is 9 miles (14 km) from north to south. Part of the Stonehenge World Heritage Site falls within it near the garrison town of Larkhill.

Surprisingly to many, the ownership of the Plain is the sole reason why this part of southern England is such an important archaeological landscape. The deep ploughing and intensive agricultural techniques that have been used on the other chalk downlands were not used on the army estate, resulting in the survival of wonderful stretches of archaeological earthworks and other remains.

Perhaps the most impressive relate to the prehistoric and Romano-British periods, and the Plain includes some staggering survivals. There are no less than twenty-seven long barrows on the Training Area. These monuments date to the early

The Salisbury Plain landscape has the most
extensive archaeological landscape in Wiltshire

Neolithic (*c*4000–3500 BC) and mid Neolithic (*c*3500–2900 BC) and are some of the earliest monuments or constructions ever built in this country. They are funerary monuments – but were not simply used for burial. Archaeologists have inferred that they were probably used for ancestor worship, which appears to have involved complicated rites with the exhumed bones of ancestors. One long barrow on the Plain which is accessible is the White Barrow near Tilshead. Another monument from this very early period is Robin Hood's Ball, a causewayed

Battlesbury hillfort

enclosure. Such monuments appear to have acted as focal points for Neolithic communities, and it is noteworthy that pottery from Cornwall and stone axes from the Lake District have been found here. The later Neolithic (c2900–2500 BC) is represented by the monuments found in and around the Stonehenge World Heritage Site such as Woodhenge and Durrington Walls.

The Plain contains a number of Bronze Age barrow cemeteries dating to the earlier Bronze Age (2500–1200 BC). Some of the best preserved barrow cemeteries in the country exist here at Silk Hill, Cow Down and Snail Down. A little later in the middle Bronze Age the Plain became heavily used by farmers and extensive 'Celtic' field systems cover many of the chalk downs. Many of these continued in use for centuries if not millennia, throughout the Iron Age (c750 BC–AD 43) when a number of massive hillforts such as Battlesbury, Bratton (an English Heritage free site), Scratchbury, Sidbury and Casterley were built.

The survival of remains from the Romano-British period (c AD 43–400) is equally impressive. Most unusually, the remains of Roman villages and their central streets still survive, defined by the earthwork remains of buildings flanking the streets. The Plain was apparently heavily used at this period for arable agriculture – perhaps providing grain for the Roman Army.

These and other remains make up a truly remarkable and extensive archaeological landscape. Monuments and sites exist over much of the Training Estate, and despite the intensive military use of the Plain, the army continues to manage its estate successfully so as to preserve them, and the highly important flora and fauna which also exist here.

Above: Male Chalkhill Blue found on Salisbury Plain

Parts of the Plain can be visited when there is no live firing. Rights of way are shown on Ordnance Survey maps, and you are urged to read and act upon the instructions provided on site notice boards by the Ministry of Defence for your own safety. Further information on access to MOD land can be found on-line at www.defence-estates.mod.uk

The layout of Ludgershall Castle can still be clearly seen

History

In its prime, Ludgershall Castle was a place of some importance. It is known to have passed into the hands of the crown by the early 12th century and was adopted by King John (1199–1216) as a useful stopping point on the road to the West Country. John probably provided Ludgershall with the strong tower that remains the most conspicuous feature of the site today. He evidently took a personal interest in developing the site as records show that he required a fireplace big enough to roast two or three oxen.

John's son, Henry III (1216–72), was a passionate enthusiast for building. The royal accounts are full of payments for improvements to his many residences, including Ludgershall. Additional rooms were provided for Henry's expanding household. King John's tower became a private chamber (solar) linked to an adjoining hall, identified by its central open hearth. No attempt seems to have been made to add to the castle's defences, since Ludgershall was more of a palatial hunting lodge than a fortress, built by the hunting forest of Savernake.

Later kings favoured Savernake less and so Ludgershall gradually fell out of use. By the 16th century it was totally ruined.

Description

The grass-grown defences of Ludgershall Castle give little clue about their former appearance.

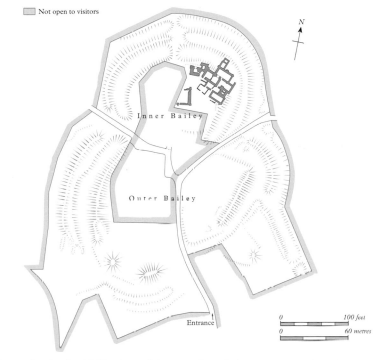

Not open to visitors

N

Inner Bailey

Outer Bailey

Entrance

0   100 *feet*

0   60 *metres*

 Plan of the castle

Excavation in the 1960s showed that today's ramparts are in fact the slumped remains of massive timber fortifications that were packed tight with earth to provide solidity against battering rams. The vertical face-timbers may even have been rendered over and limewashed to create the illusion of stonework. A modern working farm occupies the middle of the castle but the original outline, with the inner and outer

77

Ludgershall Castle Period ?II
late 14th C Peter Dunn 95

A reconstruction drawing of the castle

Above: A medieval hearth

Left: Ludgershall cross

rebuilt in stone survive today and even these have been robbed of their original facings, leaving a flint-speckled aspect quite different from their original smooth-fronted appearance. The most prominent surviving feature is the tower which dates to the late 12th century and, alongside it, the hall. The northern enclosure was excavated between 1964 and 1971 and revealed the development of various defensive and residential buildings, in both timber and stone, during the 11th to 12th centuries. A large timber-lined cellar and a dewpond were among the three phases of 12th-century buildings uncovered in the southern enclosure.

Beyond the castle entrance, faint traces of earth banks and ditches mark the outline of the medieval market town street plan. The stone cross in the main street has deep, very weathered carvings; similar crosses were erected in many market towns and were often the place where deals were struck.

baileys arranged in a figure of eight plan, can be seen clearly. The northern bailey, or ringwork, encloses an area of 4.2 acres (1.7 ha) and appears to have been inserted into the larger enclosure that now forms the southern bailey. With its double bank and ditch, this enclosure covers an area of 8.6 acres (3.5 ha).

Throughout the castle's history, many of its buildings were made of timber taken from the nearby hunting forest of Savernake. Only those

Off A342, N of
Ludgershall
OS Map 184;
ref SU 264512

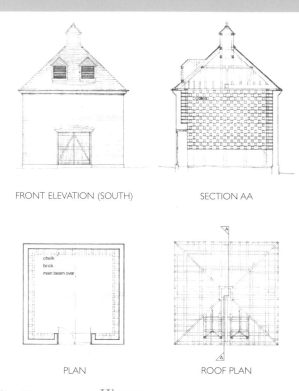

FRONT ELEVATION (SOUTH)

SECTION AA

PLAN

chalk
brick
main beam over

ROOF PLAN

Plan of the dovecote

History

The earliest dovecotes were probably built in the Middle East over 4,000 years ago. Although the Romans are known to have reared pigeons, there is no evidence that they introduced them to Britain. It is more likely that they were another introduction of the Norman nobility and, indeed, pigeons and dovecotes are mentioned in the Domesday Book of 1086. Other documentary and archaeological evidence suggests that they were used extensively by the Normans. Because construction of a dovecote was one of the privileges associated with lordship, they are often found near castles and manor houses. By the middle of the 17th century there were more than 25,000 of them in England alone. Always the preserve of the nobility, it was not until 1761 that tenant farmers were allowed to build their own dovecotes and then only with their landlord's permission. Poaching was no doubt rife especially as, with their voracious appetite for corn, pigeons must have been a curse to many farmers.

Dovecotes were a 'living larder' like large fish-ponds (stews) that were also a feature of medieval life. Doves were a source of fresh meat in winter and also provided eggs and fertiliser.

Description

Netheravon dovecote is an excellent example of an early 18th-century dovecote. It is typical of its period with a tiled pyramid-shaped roof with two dormers on the south side and is topped by a wooden lantern with a ball finial. Although it is not possible to enter the building, the interior, which still contains the majority of its original 700 chalk nesting boxes, may be seen through the slatted entrance doors. It is often said that the best-looking buildings are those whose design exactly reflects their function. Certainly the Netheravon dovecote, despite its very practical purpose, manages to be simple, elegant and an ornament to its surroundings.

Exterior viewing only
In Netheravon, 4½ miles N of Amesbury on A345
OS Map 184; ref SU 147484

Aerial view of the Sanctuary

History

The site was first recorded by John Aubrey in 1648 when many of the stones were still standing. He claimed that the Sanctuary was the name given to the site by the local people. A century later William Stukeley recorded the site shortly before it was destroyed by a farmer. In 1930 Maud Cunnington used Stukeley's drawings to rediscover it and carried out extensive excavations.

The function of the Sanctuary remains a mystery, although a number of clues suggest possible uses of the structure. The choice of site might have been made because it had traditional importance. The original wooden building may have been the home of a wise man, for example. Whatever the original significance of the site it seems to have been the centre of some type of mortuary practice. Huge numbers of human bones were found and recorded by earlier antiquaries and more fragments were found in the 1930s excavations, scattered in the soil, together with much evidence of food. This suggests that the rituals that took place in the successive buildings on the site were accompanied by elaborate feasts involving animals and a great range of ceramic vessels. The burial of a child in a crouched position along with a beaker appears to have been one of the last acts on the site before its abandonment in around 2000 BC. It seems likely that the Sanctuary was a special ritual place associated with death rites and ceremonies. In its later phases it probably took on a different character, since it was incorporated in the Avebury complex. The building of

the West Kennet Avenue in order to connect Avebury with the Sanctuary, reinforced the status of the site and allowed the new Avebury henge to share in its status and rituals. Some people have suggested that the henge represented fertility rituals whereas death rituals continued to be celebrated at the Sanctuary. Whatever its use, its importance in the ceremonial landscape is obvious and the site intriguing.

Description

Sadly, little remains of this once impressive monument, although its position within the ceremonial landscape of Avebury is clear. Now only small rectangular

blocks of concrete indicate the positions of the holes once occupied by the wooden posts and sarsen stones that formed the concentric circles of this mysterious structure.

The Sanctuary was first constructed in around 3000 BC and its site might have been a new clearing on Overton Hill or it might already have been regarded as of ceremonial importance. The first structure was a small and simply constructed round hut, measuring 15 ft (4.5 m) in diameter. There were eight posts supporting the outer wall and a single central post supporting what might have been a conical thatched roof. The second phase of

Concrete blocks marking the position of the original wooden posts and stones

83

PHASE 1

PHASE 2

PHASE 3

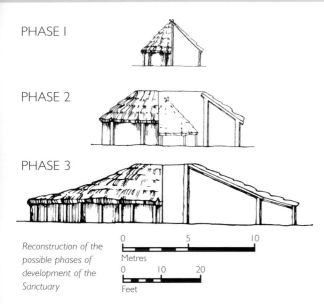

Reconstruction of the possible phases of development of the Sanctuary

0 5 10
Metres
0 10 20
Feet

On A4 near
Silbury Hill
OS Map 173;
ref SU 118680

Neolithic period owing to the pottery found in association with the post holes. This was almost twice as large as its predecessor and had a diameter of 66 ft (20 m) and three concentric rings of post holes.

At some stage, possibly while the building was still standing, a sarsen stone circle was incorporated as part of the middle ring of posts, making a near continuous internal wall of stones and posts. An entrance marked by two particularly massive posts was located on the north-west side looking roughly towards Avebury.

The fourth and last phase of construction appears to be contemporary with the West Kennet Avenue and possibly with the stone circles at Avebury. It consisted of a sarsen stone circle of forty-two stones erected to form an outer boundary to the Sanctuary complex. This circle was 138 ft (40 m) in diameter and was connected to the West Kennet Avenue by two stones on the circumference, in roughly the same position as the door posts of the previous phase.

building, perhaps 100 to 200 years later, saw a new extended building on the same site, which completely enclosed the first hut (probably still standing) within a much larger structure. There were two rings of post holes, very much larger in size than the first hut, with a diameter of 37 ft (11.2 m). The third phase appears to belong to the later

Silbury Hill was built in several phases and there are several mounds now buried beneath the final one. Recent radiocarbon dates from an excavation by English Heritage at the top of the hill place the date of the final mound's construction at *c* BC 2500–2350. By that time the Avebury area had already been a ritual centre for hundreds of years.

After the great period of Neolithic Avebury, which perhaps ended around 1800 BC, the ritual landscape gradually fell into disuse. The Romans exploited the hill in a novel way, using it for sighting their new road from Mildenhall to Bath: at Silbury itself the road had to make a kink, linking the two straight sections on either side. In the Saxon period the hill appears to have been used as a lookout post, and it is possible that the summit was fortified. Certainly excavation in 1968–9 showed the whole top area to be disturbed, perhaps both from Saxon fortification and from the work of earlier antiquaries.

Left: Aerial view of the hill

Below*: A stag's antler found during excavations at Silbury Hill*

History

Silbury Hill is the largest man-made mound in Europe, covering an area of 5½ acres (2.2 ha). At 130 ft (40 m) high, and with a volume of 12.5 million cubic ft (350,000 cubic m), it is comparable in size to the pyramids of Egypt, with which it is roughly contemporary. It is assumed that at least 1,000 men were involved – an extraordinary feat of cooperation for early farming communities with no written form of communication. Estimates of the time taken to build the hill vary from two to ten years, depending on the length of time that the workforce could be assembled for.

Silbury Hill — dramatic in all seasons. Covered in snow it seems to float above the landscape

A skeleton was discovered in 1723 during tree planting on the summit and items buried with it suggest that it also dated from this period.

Numerous investigations have failed to reveal anything within the mound, such as a burial or a symbolic hoard or shrine, and it therefore seems likely that Silbury Hill was important in itself, not for what it contained. The exact purpose of the site, however, remains a mystery.

Description

In plan, the base is octagonal, while the flat top is roughly square in shape.

An original construction terrace remains visible near the top but the various terraces dug out from the sides post-date its Neolithic construction.

Shafts dug both from the summit and the sides of the hill have revealed the full complexity of the construction. It appears that initially a mound of around 130 ft (40 m) in diameter was constructed on a natural chalk spur. It was subsequently twice enlarged by digging a surrounding ditch which had the effect of reducing the spur and thus exaggerating the height of the mound. The construction was a very careful one, using layers of chalk rubble contained by walls of larger chalk blocks. These formed huge terraces about 16 ft (5 m) high that were later filled in with river silt to produce the present outline. It is possible that these 'terraces' were, in fact, originally constructed as a spiral ramp giving access to the summit. The finished hill would have looked something like a rounded white version of a Sumerian ziggurat. It has proved to be a very strong construction,

although recent slippage has meant that no access can be allowed on to the hill itself for safety reasons. The surrounding ditch, once 20 ft (6 m) deep and 70 ft (21 m) wide has now silted up. The immense amount of material required was obtained from the ditch, from the original hill slope that ran through the base of the mound and from local quarrying. Silbury Hill has been designated a Historic Engineering Work by the Institute of Civil Engineers – the oldest monument on their register.

Drawing by William Stukeley, 1723

1 mile of West Kennet on A4
No access on to the hill itself; viewing area any reasonable time
OS Map 173; ref SU 100685

87

The large sarsen stones of the Avenue

History

The Avenue was erected sometime after the initial construction of Avebury and the Sanctuary, suggesting a changing relationship between the older monuments. As well as marking the route, the stones seem to have acted as grave markers for some members of the Avebury community. Some time after the Avenue was erected, several shallow burials were placed at the foot of the stones. In the 1930s Alexander Keiller, heir to the Keiller marmalade fortune, excavated four graves, all belonging to the Beaker period (*c* 2500–1800 BC); three contained a single person, but the fourth had the remains of three. These were particularly important people or, possibly, they were buried as sacrificial offerings in some form of ancestor worship. Elsewhere along the Avenue, excavations revealed scatters of human bone, presumably also from burials. Many of the stones had already disappeared by the time the first record of the Avenue was made, by John Aubrey, in the 17th century. William Stukeley, in the following century, left an account of the massive destruction of the standing stone monuments of Avebury. They were being torn down and broken into fragments for building material. Alexander Keiller was able to demonstrate that the practice of burying the stones had happened since the Middle Ages when they were possibly associated with pagan worship and considered the work of the devil. Stukeley recorded a similar avenue on the Beckhampton side of the Avebury henge but little of this remains today.

Description

Originally, the Avenue consisted of around 100 pairs of standing stones.

These created a corridor 49 ft (15 m) wide along the entirety of the winding 1½ mile (2.5 km) course. Each pair of stones stood about 80 ft (24.5 m) from the next. The sarsen stones used are not quite as large as those at Avebury and average about 10 ft (3 m) high. They appear to have been selected for their shape; some are long and cylindrical, while others are broad and often triangular in shape. Generally, stones of the two different types stood opposite each other. It has been suggested that they may have been intended as male and female representations, the male being long and cylindrical and the female triangular. Today, there are twenty-seven upright stones (the sites of thirty-seven others are marked by concrete pillars), largely thanks to the efforts of Alexander Keiller whose excavations resulted in their being found and re-erected.

The course of the Avenue appears to take little regard of the natural contours of the area and, on first sight, there seems little logic behind

the choice of the route. The discovery and excavation of a Neolithic site that the Avenue skirts, however, suggests that the curves and bends in its course may well have respected existing settlements and buildings.

Above. An 18th-century engraving of West Kennet Avenue

Left: The Avenue

Alongside
B4003
OS Map 173;
ref SU 105695

Above: Massive stones at the entrance to the barrow

including pottery, beads and stone implements such as a dagger, dated to between 3000 and 2600 BC. The tomb was closed sometime around 2000 BC and the main passage filled with earth, stones, rubble and debris. The forecourt was then blocked with sarsen boulders and a false entrance of twin sarsen uprights constructed. Finally, three massive sarsen blocking-stones were erected across the front (eastern end) of the tomb. The barrow was first excavated in 1859 and then again, scientifically, in 1955–6, after

History

One of the largest and most impressive Neolithic graves in Britain, West Kennet long barrow was built in around 3400 BC and used for at least 1,000 years. It may have been constructed in at least two phases, as there is a noticeable bulge halfway along the longitudinal axis accompanied by a subtle change in direction. Some cremations and the partial remains of at least forty-six individuals – both male and female and of all ages – have been found inside, together with grave goods

Right: Aerial view of the long barrow

Left: View into the barrow interior

which the site was restored and the façade and chambers at the eastern end reconstructed.

Description

The huge earth barrow survives to a maximum height of 10 ft 6 in (3.2 m) and tapers out from the narrower western end to a maximum width of 82 ft (25 m) towards the eastern entrance. At just over 328 ft (100 m), the barrow is second only to the nearby East Kennet Barrow in length. Although it is now covered with turf it would originally have had bare chalk sides and would have stood out against the landscape. It consists of a core of sarsen stones capped with chalk rubble from the surrounding quarry ditches.

At the eastern end of the mound is an impressive structure consisting of five chambers opening off a central passage. This is fronted by a semi-circular forecourt with a façade of huge sarsen stones aligned in a north–south direction. The main passage penetrates about 42 ft (13 m) into the barrow, with two of the burial chambers on each side of the passageway and one chamber at the end. The side ditches to the north and south of the mound have now been almost buried by ploughing. It is possible to enter the chamber of the barrow, and from the top of the mound there are good views of Silbury Hill, the East Kennet Barrow, the Sanctuary and Windmill Hill.

¼ mile SW of West Kennet, along footpath off A4
OS Map 173; ref SU 105677

Right: A
*reconstruction
drawing of a burial
ceremony at the
rectangular enclosure*

History

Windmill Hill is famous for being one of the first sites excavated to provide evidence of the life of early farming communities in southern Britain. It is also the largest of all known causewayed enclosure sites in Britain. Its discovery and preservation is due to Alexander Keiller. He bought most of the site in the 1920s (saving it from Marconi, the wireless pioneers, who planned to build a relay station on the summit) and carried out meticulous excavations until the Second World War. His finds came mainly from the three concentric ditches and included flint tools and fragments of early pottery, together with human and animal bones, including the intact skeleton of a young child. Many of these objects can now be seen in the Alexander Keiller Museum at Avebury.

From Keiller's discoveries, and later investigations, it seems that Windmill Hill was occupied and cultivated even before 3000 BC, when the enclosure was constructed, and remained in use until around 2500 BC.

The massive effort of digging the three ditches seems to have happened rather spasmodically, perhaps in slack periods of the agricultural year, and perhaps by several different local groups. It has been estimated that at least 62,000 hours were spent in the construction, undertaken over several years as successive ditches were added. Large numbers of cattle and sheep were killed or eaten on the site and it is possible that it might have been a place to hold festivals, or a market where animals were slaughtered and artefacts traded. Alternatively, it could have been a site where ritual feasts were held. Perhaps it was all of these things.

The rectangular enclosure to the east, contemporary with the circular ditches, has been interpreted as a mortuary enclosure. This was where human corpses were left to be picked clean of flesh, prior to the ritual interment of the skull and principal bones in a chambered tomb such as that of West Kennet nearby.

Description

Three concentric rings of ditches circle the hilltop, enclosing an area of 21 acres (8.5 ha). None of these ditches is continuous as they are broken at intervals by crossing points – hence the term 'causewayed'. Each ditch would once have been fronted by a bank, though most of these have now disappeared, either through

falling back into the ditch or more recent ploughing. From the end of the third millennium BC, Windmill Hill seems to have been largely abandoned. It is possible that a folk memory of the former importance of the site lived on, since the summit of the site later became the focus of a Bronze Age cemetery. The remains of these great tumuli can still be seen although there is little information about their structure or contents.

Aerial photography showing the barrow outlines

1½ miles NW
of Avebury
OS Map 173;
ref SU 087714

History

Woodhenge is an atmospheric Neolithic site, probably built about 2300 BC. It was originally believed to be the remains of a large burial mound, surrounded by a bank and ditch almost completely destroyed by ploughing, but aerial photography detected rings of dark spots in a crop of wheat. When the site was excavated these proved to be empty sockets that had formerly held large upright timbers. The timbers in the third ring seem to have been larger and more deeply set than the others, so the posts may have been the uprights of a large roofed building with a small courtyard or light-well in the centre. It is also quite possible that the site was completely open to the sky with the posts carved and painted like totem poles. It is impossible to know for certain what the rings of timbers were for. One clue was the discovery at the centre of the site of the burial of a three-year-old child whose skull had been split open with an axe – apparently a human sacrifice. A structure similar to Woodhenge may have stood at the centre of Stonehenge before the great stone circle and trilithons were erected; traces of two more have been found within the large enclosure known as Durrington Walls that lies just 230 ft (70 m) to the north of Woodhenge. The exact appearance, purpose and status of these structures remains unknown. If they were indeed roofed buildings, they may have

Right: Symbolic chalk axes excavated at Woodhenge

Below: The shape of Woodhenge revealed by aerial photography

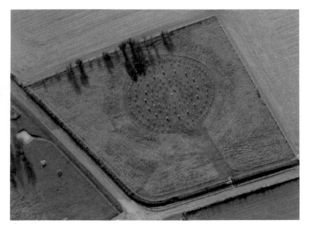

served many functions, just as parish churches did in the Middle Ages. It appears that structures like Woodhenge mark a particular stage in the evolution in human religious belief and community organisation – one that was to achieve its final and most permanent form at Stonehenge nearby. Radiocarbon dating of finds from within the henge, indicates that it was still in use around 1800 BC. During the Iron Age and Roman periods evidence of later settlement in the immediate vicinity demonstrates continued use beyond its ceremonial function. It is possible that the banks and ditches were used for defensive purposes.

Description

There are six concentric rings of post holes which are marked today by concrete blocks. The rings are oval-shaped, with the longer axis pointing towards the winter and summer solstice. The circular bank and ditch surrounding the rings covered an area measuring 360 ft (110 m) in diameter overall with a single entrance to the north-east. Although these are hardly visible on the ground now, excavations in 1926–8 revealed that the bank was about 33 ft (10 m) wide and that the ditch is flat bottomed, up to 40 ft (12 m) wide and 8 ft (2.4 m) deep.

A reconstruction showing how Woodhenge might have looked in Neolithic times

1½ miles N of Amesbury off A345, just S of Durrington

OS Map 184; ref SU 151434

Five English Heritage sites in this area are staffed and most have a separate guidebook, which can be purchased at the site's gift shop or by mail order. These sites charge an admission fee, although admission is free to members of English Heritage (see inside back cover). **Please note that sites listed here as opening on 1 April open at Easter if it falls earlier.** Full details of admission charges, access and opening times for all of English Heritage's sites are given in the *English Heritage Members' and Visitors' Handbook*, and on our website (www.english-heritage.org.uk).

Details of English Heritage publications can be found in the Publications Catalogue. To obtain a free copy of the catalogue, and to order English Heritage publications, please contact:

English Heritage Postal Sales
c/o Gillards, Trident Works
Temple Cloud, Bristol BS39 5AZ

Tel: 01761 452966 Fax: 01761 453408
E-mail: ehsales@gillards.com

ALEXANDER KEILLER MUSEUM
WILTSHIRE

This fascinating museum contains one of the most important prehistoric archaeological collections in Britain. The admission fee includes access to the Barn Gallery which reveals the story of the landscape and its people over the past 6,000 years. The museum collection is managed by the National Trust.

Open all year except 24–25 Dec
In Avebury, 7 miles W of Marlborough

HAILES ABBEY
GLOUCESTERSHIRE

Founded in 1246 by Richard, Earl of Cornwall, the son of King John, this Cistercian abbey was built on a lavish scale, and later gained great importance by the gift of a phial of the Holy Blood in 1270 which brought pilgrims flocking to Hailes. To house the relic the east end of the church was rebuilt on an elaborate polygonal plan. After the suppression in 1539, the south and west cloistral buildings survived as a country house for nearly two centuries. By the Victorian period the site had been abandoned and was so overgrown that its exact location was uncertain. Today the beautifully restored ruins of this important abbey still evoke an atmosphere of peace and serenity.

Open 1 Apr–31 Oct daily. Please call for admission prices and opening times: 01242 602398.

2 miles NE of Winchcombe off B4632
OS Map 150; ref SP 050300

OLD SARUM
WILTSHIRE

This great earthwork built by Iron-Age peoples was later occupied by Romans, Saxons and Normans. It was here that William the Conqueror paid off his army in 1070, and a castle, palace and cathedral were built inside the earthwork. When New Sarum, the city we know as Salisbury, was founded in 1226, the settlement began to decline but the castle remained in use until the Tudor period. The remains of the prehistoric fortress, Norman palace, castle and cathedral are powerful reminders of thousands of years of history.

Open all year except 24–26 Dec and 1 Jan. Please call for admission prices and opening times: 01722 335398

2 miles N of Salisbury off A345
OS Map 184; ref SU 138327

OLD WARDOUR CASTLE
WILTSHIRE

One of the most romantic ruins in England, set in elaborate landscaped gardens this six-sided castle was built in the 14th century for John, 5th Lord Lovel. It was designed in the French style popular at the time and built on a lavish scale to impress everyone with Lovel's power and taste. Although badly damaged during the English Civil War, the castle was restored by the Arundell family who continued to maintain it as a ruin when they built New Wardour nearby in 1776.

Open all year except 24–26 Dec and 1 Jan; Nov – Easter weekends only. Please call for admission prices and opening times: 01747 870487

Located off A30 2 miles SW of Tisbury
OS Map 184; ref ST 939263

STONEHENGE
WILTSHIRE

The great stone circle of Stonehenge is one of the wonders of the world. What visitors see today are the substantial remnants of the last in a sequence of such monuments erected between *c* 3000 BC and 1600 BC. Although there has always been debate about its purpose, it is clear that Stonehenge was the focal point in a landscape filled with prehistoric ceremonial structures. Now a World Heritage Site, Stonehenge and all its surroundings remain powerful witnesses to the once great civilisations of the Stone and Bronze Ages between 5,000 and 3,000 years ago.

Open all year except 24–26 Dec and 1 Jan.
Please call for admission prices and opening times:
01980 624715

2 miles W of Amesbury on junction A303 and A344/A360
OS Map 184; ref SU 122422

INDEX

INDEX

FURTHER READING

BRISTOL

Temple Church

Temple Church, Bristol. Salisbury: Wessex Archaeology, 2000

GLOUCESTERSHIRE

Belas Knap Long Barrow

Grinsell, L V *Belas Knap Long Barrow*, 2nd edn. London: HMSO, 1978

Blackfriars

Morely, B M *Blackfriars, Gloucester*. Scotland: HMSO, 1979

Cirencester Amphitheatre

Beecham, K J *History of Cirencester and the Roman city Corinium*. Alan Sutton, 1978

Viner, D J *The surviving mouments of Corinium: the Roman Cirencester*. Cirencester: Corinium Museum, 1973

Great Witcombe Roman Villa

Leach, P, Bevan, L and Pearson, T *Great Witcombe Roman Villa, Gloucestershire: a report on excavations by Ernest Greenfield 1960–1973*. Oxford: British Archaeological Reports, 1978

Neal, D S 'Witcombe Roman Villa [Gloucestershire] a reconstruction'. *Ancient monuments and their interpretation; essays presented to A.J. Taylor*, pp 27-40

Greyfriars

Ferris, I M 'Excavations at Greyfriars, Gloucester in 1967 and 1974–5'. *Transactions of the Bristol and Gloucestershire Archaeological Society*, vol 119 (2001), pp 95–146

Kingswood Abbey Gatehouse

Arnold, A J, Howard, R E and Litton, C D *Tree ring analysis of timbers from Kingswood Abbey Gatehouse, Kingswood, Gloucestershire*. Portsmouth: English Heritage Centre for Archaeology, 2003

Nympsfield Long Barrow

Saville, A 'Further excavations at Nympsfield chambered tomb, Gloucestershire'. *Proceedings of the Prehistoric Society*, vol 45, 1979, pp 53–91

Odda's Chapel

Fletcher, E *Odda's Chapel, Deerhurst, Gloucestershire*. London: HMSO, 1965

Currie, C R J 'A Romanesque roof at Odda's Chapel, Deerhurst, Gloucestershire?' *The Antiquaries Journal*, vol 63, 1983, pp 58–63

Offa's Dyke

Hill, D H 'The construction of Offa's Dyke'. *The Antiquaries Journal*, vol 65, 1985, pp 140–2

Wright, C J *A Guide to Offa's Dyke path*. 2nd edn. London: Constable, 1986

Over Bridge

Rolt, L T C *Thomas Telford*. London: Longmans, 1958

St Briavel's Castle

Remfry, P M *St Briavel's Castle, 1066 to 1331*. Malvern Link: SCS Publishing, 1994

Webb, A 'St Briavel's –the king's great arsenal'. *Dean Archaeol*, vol 5, 1992, pp 18–23

St Mary's

Gethyn-Jones, J E, *St Mary's Church, Kempley, and its paintings*, vol 1, 1961. Gloucester: John Bellows

Morley, B M, 1985, 'The nave roof of the church of St Mary, Kempley, Gloucestershire'. *The Antiquaries Journal,* vol 65, pp 101–11

Uley Long Barrow

Grinsell, L V *Hetty Pegler's Tump: Uley: Gloucestershire.* London: HMSO, 1970

WILTSHIRE

Avebury

Malone, C *The English Heritage Book of Avebury.* London: Batsford, 1989

Malone, C 1994 *The prehistoric monuments of Avebury, Wiltshire (guide),* 2nd edn. London: English Heritage, 1994

Bradford-on-Avon Tithe Barn

Ministry of Works *The mediaeval tithe barn, Bradford-on-Avon, Wiltshire (guide).* London: HMSO, 1953

Bratton Camp and White Horse

Woolner, D 'New Light on the White Horse [Uffington, Berkshire], *Folklore: Transactions of the Folklore Society,* vol 78, 1967, pp 90–112

Ludgershall Castle and Cross

Ellis, P (ed) *Ludgershall Castle, Wiltshire: A report on the excavations by Peter Addyman 1964–1972.* Devizes: Wiltshire Archaeological and Natural History Society, 2000

The Sanctuary

Pollard, J 'The Sanctuary, Overton Hill, Wiltshire: A re-examination'. *Proceedings of the Prehistoric Society,* vol 58, 1992, pp 213–26

Silbury Hill

Whittle, A *Sacred mound, holy rings. Silbury Hill and the West Kennet palisade enclosures.* Oxford: Oxbow Books, 1997

Netheravon Dovecote

Hansell, P & J *Doves and dovecotes.* Bath: Millstream Books, 1988

West Kennet Avenue

Thom, A and Strang, A 'Avebury (2): the West Kennet Avenue'. *J. Hist Astron,* vol 7, 1976, pp 193–7

West Kennet Long Barrow

Piggott, S *The West Kennet long barrow; excavations 1955–6.* London: HMSO, 1962

Woodhenge

Cunnington, M E *Woodhenge: a description of the site as revealed by excavations carried out there by Mr and Mrs B H Cunnington, 1926–7–8; also of four circles and an earthwork enclosure south of Woodhenge.* Devizes: George Simpson, 1929

FEATURES

Bristol's Architectural Heritage

Pevsner, N *North Somerset and Bristol.* Harmondsworth: Penguin, 1958

Long Barrows of Gloucestershire

Ashbee, P *The earthen long barrow in Britain: An introduction to the study of the Neolithic people of the third millennium BC,* 2nd edn. Norwich: Geo Books, 1984

FURTHER READING AND WEBSITES

The Roman Influence

McWhirr, A 1981 *Roman Gloucestershire*. Gloucester: Alan Sutton Publishing

Writers and Artists of Bristol, Gloucestershire and Wiltshire

Matthews, H and Treitel, P *The forward life of Richard Jefferies: A chronological study.* Oxford: Petton, 1994

Fraser, J L 1976 *John Constable 1776–1837: The man and his mistress.* London: Hutchinson, 1976

Hooper, B *Cider with Laurie: Laurie Lee remembered.* London: Peter Owen, 1999

Gray, P *Marginal Men: Edward Thomas, Ivor Gurney, J R Acherley.* Basingstoke: Macmillan, 1991

Groom, N (ed) *Thomas Chatterton and romantic culture.* Basingstoke: Macmillan, 1999

Brunel's Great Western Railway

Brindle, S *Paddington Station: Its history and architecture.* London: English Heritage, 2004

Semmens, P *A history of the Great Western Railway*, 3 vols. London: George Allen and Unwin, 1985

Audrey, C *Encyclopaedia of the Great Western Railway.* Sparkford: Patrick Stephens, 1993

Salisbury Plain Training Area

McOmish, D, Field, D and Brown, G *The field archaeology of the Salisbury Plain Training Area.* Swindon: English Heritage, 2002

Useful websites relating to Bristol, Gloucestershire and Wiltshire

www.english-heritage.org.uk
(English Heritage)

www.butterfly-conservation.org.uk
(Butterfly Conservation)

www.cheltenhammuseum.org.uk
(Cheltenham Museum and Art Gallery)

www.visitcheltenham.com
(Cheltenham Tourist Information)

www.britarch.ac.uk
(Council for British Archaeology)

www.cpat.org.uk
(Clwyd-Powys Archaeological Trust)

www.devizes-tc.gov.uk
(Wiltshire Heritage Museum, Devizes)

www.nationaltrust.org.uk
(National Trust)

www.swindon.gov.uk
(Richard Jefferies Museum)

www.steam-museum.org.uk
(Steam Museum, Swindon)